CHRISTIAN HERITAGE COLLEGE
2100 Greenfield Dr.
El Cajon, CA 92021

Thomas Mann

A Critical
Study

Thomas Mann

A Critical Study

R. J. Hollingdale

Rupert Hart-Davis   London

Granada Publishing Limited
First published in Great Britian 1971 by Rupert Hart-Davis Ltd
3 Upper James Street London W1R 4BP

ISBN 0 246 64037 5
Printed in Great Britain by Ebenezer Baylis & Son Ltd
The Trinity Press, Worcester, and London

I have a subtler sense for signs of ascent and decline than any man has ever had, I am the teacher *par excellence* in this matter—I know both, I am both.
NIETZSCHE: *Ecce Homo* I 1

Wofür ich Allah höchlich danke?
Dass er Leiden und Wissen getrennt.
Verzweifeln müsste jeder Kranke
Das Übel kennend wie der Arzt es kennt.
GOETHE: *West-Östlicher Divan.*
Buch der Sprüche

Contents

Foreword

In this study of Thomas Mann's novels and stories I attempt to dig down to the foundations of his fictional world and show what it rests on; to illumine its connexion with and reliance on certain outstanding figures of the German literary and philosophical tradition, especially Nietzsche; and to indicate in what way it mirrors the real world of its time, which is still our time. Each of the six central chapters discusses a particular theme; the first chapter outlines what I take to be the broad basis of the work, and the last ventures a few generalizations and speculations.

Quotations are taken from the standard translations, because these are what for the English-speaking reader constitute Thomas Mann's novels and stories, and I do not want anyone to suppose my interpretation of them depends on anything not communicated in these translations; but, except where otherwise stated, I have translated quotations from other German writers myself.

In order not to have continually to refer to dates of composition, I here give a chronological list of the novels and stories referred to in the text:

1897   Little Herr Friedemann
       The Dilettante
       Tobias Mindernickel
       Little Lizzie
1899   The Wardrobe
1901   Buddenbrooks
       The Way to the Churchyard
1902   Tristan
       Gladius Dei
1903   Tonio Kröger
       The Infant Prodigy
1905   A Weary Hour
       The Blood of the Wälsungs

1911 The Confessions of Felix Krull [Part I]
     Death in Venice
1924 The Magic Mountain
1929 Mario and the Magician
~~1933–43 Joseph and his Brothers~~
1939 Lotte in Weimar
1947 Doctor Faustus
1951 The Holy Sinner [Der Erwählte]
1953 The Black Swan [Die Betrogene]
1954 The Confessions of Felix Krull [Parts II and III]

For permission to quote from Thomas Mann's works I must thank Alfred A. Knopf, Inc. (*Joseph and his Brothers*, edition in one volume), and Martin Secker and Warburg Ltd (*Stories of Three Decades, Buddenbrooks, The Magic Mountain, Lotte in Weimar, Doctor Faustus, The Holy Sinner, Confessions of Felix Krull, The Black Swan* and *Genesis of a Novel*). I am also grateful to Penguin Books Ltd for permission to quote from my translations of Nietzsche's *Thus Spoke Zarathustra, Twilight of the Idols* and *The Anti-Christ*, and my translation of *Essays and Aphorisms* of Schopenhauer, published by them; and to quote from N. J. Dawood's translation of the Koran.

1 European Nihilism

1

The tradition in which you grow up keeps a firm hold—even when you do not know it, even when you reject and deny it. Consider the case of Thomas Mann. In the title-story of his first book he sends his outsider-hero little Herr Friedemann to a performance of *Lohengrin*; the force of this music, combined with that of the immediate proximity of the evil Frau von Rinnlingen, proves too much for him; the dam of repression which he has all his life been erecting in the path of his sexuality is broken down; and he goes forward to hysteria, madness and death. Nothing, it might seem, could differ more completely from this story than Mann's last literary project, upon which he was engaged at the very end of his life, a full sixty years after little Herr Friedemann had met his doom: a play on the subject of Luther's wedding. But they do possess at least one element in common. Wagner sketched out a drama on the theme of Luther's wedding in August 1868—an after-echo, certainly, of the *Meistersinger*, which had received its first performance the previous June.[1] Mann knew, of course, that Wagner had preceded him in reflecting on the dramatic possibilities of the marriage of a monk and a nun, and I have no doubt it was that which first drew his attention to the subject: that is to say, his Luther-project belonged within the ambit of his Wagner-interest. Wagner at the beginning, Wagner at the end: it is a useful symbol of Thomas Mann's loyalty to his tradition.

He often declared he had broken with this tradition—or rather, to quote one of his formulations of the nature of this breach, that his 'moral horizon' had broadened during the First World War to include 'the European-democratic religion of humanity', whereas it had previously been 'bounded solely by late German romanticism, by Schopenhauer, Nietzsche, Wagner'.[2] But I would call this a slight case of self-misunderstanding, and not a unique one among artists who reflect on their own evolution. The phrase which speaks of the 'religion of humanity' might have been uttered by Settembrini (perhaps *was* uttered by him, for no one can remember every word spoken by the voluble invalid), and I hope to convince the reader that Settembrini, though drawn with love and humour, is, together with his religion of humanity, finally rejected and reduced to farce by his creator. Moreover, since it is made to include Nietzsche, 'late German romanticism' is also misunderstood, and misunderstood in a way in which Mann as a creative artist never misunderstood it. When he speaks in his own proper person, he tells us (if one may judge by his actions) the truth about what he is thinking; but if, when we read his novels and stories, we find he there says something different, we must refuse to believe he is really saying what he says in his own proper person; we must assert that, if his words are intended to apply to his art-works, he is misreporting himself, and set him out of court as an incompetent witness on the familiar and undisputed ground that what an artist says he said is not evidence. In his place we must seek testimony from the Buddenbrook family and the inmates of Haus Berghof, from Joseph and his brothers and Adrian and his biographer, from Cipolla and Felix Krull, and from as many more of that company of masks as we shall require. And we must also feel ourselves free to call on the *other* Thomas Mann: I mean the artist immersed, sometimes years-long, in a work of art through which he may at any time tell us truths about himself without necessarily realizing it.

2

What does Thomas Mann, novelist and storyteller, write about? With a large exception (which will not be overlooked) he writes about European men and women in a condition of physical decay and mental confusion and moral uncertainty. He depicts the decline of a family and the neurotic isolation of exceptional individuals within the normal world; he describes incest in Berlin and death in Venice and life in a Swiss sanatorium; he paints a corrupt and darkened continent in which the only light is the light of genius, and then wants us to see that this light is only the phosphorescence of corruption. He is obsessed with illness. How many different forms of illness are described in his books? I have not counted them: scores, certainly, and many are delineated with minute and scientific exactitude. And throughout, always there if not always explicit, is the feeling that it is not merely this or that individual but a whole civilization of which the individual is a representative case, which is sick and done for. The family which declines is not merely the Buddenbrooks, it is the European family. What, then, is (excluding that large exception) Thomas Mann's subject? It is a detailed description of *European nihilism* — and by that (to define at once a word so equivocal in meaning) I mean the breakdown of European civilization as predicted and diagnosed by the one figure belonging to Mann's tradition capable of such a prediction and diagnosis. The Europe to be discovered in Mann's fiction, and the tenor of the way in which he describes it, is to be accounted for and explained by comparing it with Nietzsche's reflections on the state of this continent and its people; what he has to say about them is finally comprehensible only as a consequence of what Nietzsche had to say in different words and in another idiom.

The tradition in which Mann consciously placed himself but which he said he had subsequently stepped beyond he summarized in the names Schopenhauer, Wagner and Nietzsche, but there is clearly also a fourth figure which he failed to mention in association with the other three because he did not care to assert that he had passed beyond him, and this is of course Goethe. He wrote famous essays on all four but, more importantly, their names, or allusions to them, or the titles of their works, also appear many times in his novels and stories, and we shall encounter them constantly. The series Goethe, Schopenhauer, Wagner, Nietzsche at first seemed to Mann to constitute a logical, or at any rate cultural succession, but we shall discover that this series was unstable and broke apart, with Goethe leading in one direction and Schopenhauer and Wagner leading in another, while Nietzsche came to predominate as the decisive figure. It then becomes apparent that Mann's view of Goethe, Schopenhauer and Wagner had in reality always been more or less identical with Nietzsche's view of them, though he was certainly not always aware of that fact. Mann believed he had stepped beyond this tradition: what had happened in reality is that this tradition had turned upon itself in the person of Nietzsche and, through his

13

instrumentality, shown itself up—so that Mann is finally able to feel superior to it without actually being outside it.

The question to be answered is still and always: Why? Life as it appears in most of Mann's books is not life as it appears to most people: it is far more uncanny, far more questionable and uncertain, far more sick, far *worse*. Why is that so? Why does life appear like that in most of Thomas Mann's books? My answer is: because his subject turns out on examination to be a detailed description of that European nihilism previously defined by Nietzsche.

3

Suppose a civilization has been created and educated essentially and at bottom by its religion, so that in so far as the life of its people possesses direction, purpose and meaning it is their religion which has bestowed these things upon it: what will happen to that civilization when its religion ceases to be believed in? And suppose further that this religion has preached and inculcated before all else the sacredness of truth, declaring itself to be 'the truth': what will happen when the fidelity to truth thus inculcated compels the people of that civilization to deny that its religion is 'the truth'? The answer is that there will occur a kind of somersault in the realm of values, so that the sometime paradox 'The truth is that there is no truth' will become actuality and a historical force, while the direction, purpose and meaning formerly bestowed on life by religion will become paradoxes.

This state of things is what Nietzsche declared was in store for Europe once it had become fully conscious that it had lost its religion: the highest values—direction, purpose, meaning and truth—would 'disvalue themselves', and thereafter 'the belief that there is no truth whatever, the nihilists' belief',[3] would become a cultural fact.

Nietzsche's work is filled with a sense of this coming nihilistic collapse of values, and he took it for a certainty because he had thought his way through it and believed his conclusions unavoidable. 'What I relate,' he said, 'is the history of the next two centuries. I describe what is coming, what can no longer come otherwise: *the rise of nihilism*.'[4] His own 'revaluation of all values' he considered a 'counter-

14

movement' to this collapse but one that presupposed it and could come 'only after it and out of it. For why is the rise of nihilism now a *necessity?* Because it is the very values we have had hitherto which draw their final conclusion in nihilism; because nihilism is the ultimate logical end of our great values and ideals—because we must first experience nihilism before we can discover what the real value of these "values" has been...'[5] Asking 'What does nihilism mean?' he answered: '*That the supreme values disvalue themselves.* The goal is lacking. The answer is lacking to the question "Why? to what purpose?" '[6] And in a similar formulation he asserted that 'the whole *idealism* of mankind hitherto is on the point of turning suddenly into *nihilism*—into the belief in absolute *value*lessness, i.e. *meaning*lessness'.[7]

The old beliefs were going out and taking with them all the old certainties; and Nietzsche was occupied in book after book in demonstrating what could follow from that. If you cease to believe in the Creation story and adhere instead to a belief in evolution, you cannot help depriving mankind of the special position in the universe it formerly held, but will be compelled to see that the concepts and qualities in which mankind takes pride are reducible to a few simple qualities in which, on the basis of existing taste, it is impossible to take pride. You will be compelled to see that rationality is based on irrationality, into the darkness of which it ultimately disappears, and that morality is by its own tenets immorality. You will have to admit that the 'higher' world, the metaphysical, derives from the human, which is as much as to say that it ceases to exist. You will have to acknowledge that 'God is dead',[8] and that with him the 'godlike' in man has also expired, that 'humanity, humaneness and "human dignity" ' are illusions born of error.[9] There will no longer be any reason left for you to believe that the universe is *directed*—by God or by any other ordering principle: you will have to see that 'its total nature... is...to all eternity chaos'.[10] If you cease to believe in God you will not be excused from drawing the consequences of this loss of belief, and civilization will then experience a 'decay of cosmological values': 'the categories "purpose", "unity", "being" by means of which we have injected a value into the world, will be *extracted* again—and now the world seems *valueless*'.[11] Consciousness of this decline in values has been growing for a long time: 'Since Copernicus man seems to have got himself on to an inclined plane – now he is sliding faster and faster away from the centre – whither? into nothingness? into a *"penetrating* sense of his nothingness"?'[12] But the climax and cataclysm are at hand: a complete loss of faith in the ideals by which Europe has hitherto sustained itself, in the values hitherto supreme, and the consequent disappearance of all *meaning* – this is what Nietzsche prognosticated for European civilization, and he was shaken by the conviction it was coming suddenly and coming soon.

What I would assert is that Mann's novels and stories depict the European continent declining into this condition of nihilistic loss of values; and that what appears to be his conception of the *cause* of this decline is not only among the most prominent and characteristic of his themes but also identical with Nietzsche's conception of its cause.

4

The most fateful consequence of this disappearance of absolute values – in Nietzsche's view and also from the point of view of common sense – is that *moral* values cease to be categorical. This is the effect which threatens the greatest practical harm and an actual dehumanization of humanity. 'Skepticism regarding morality is what is decisive. The decline of the *moral* interpretation of the world, which no longer has any *sanction* after it has sought to escape into a Beyond, ends in nihilism. "Nothing has any meaning"...'[13] The reason this is so is that 'the Christian moral hypothesis' possessed certain advantages which its relinquishment has done away with: 'it lent man an absolute *value*, in antithesis to his smallness and contingency in the flux of becoming and passing away; it served the advocates of God, insofar as it allowed to the world, in spite of suffering and evil, the character of *perfection*...evil appeared full of *meaning*;...it prevented man from despising himself as man, from taking sides against life...: it was a *means of preservation*...morality was the great *antidote* against practical and theoretical *nihilism*'.[14] The disappearance of categorical morality is an instance of that paradoxical *self-devaluation* of values: '*Radical nihilism* is the conviction of an absolute untenability of existence when it comes to the highest values one recognizes; plus the *insight* that we have not the slightest right to posit a Beyond or an in-itself of things that might be "divine", morality incarnate. This insight is a consequence of the cultivation of "truthfulness": thus itself a consequence of belief in morality.'[15]

Disbelief in the Christian religion, Nietzsche asserts, must mean the end of categorical morality: 'They [the English] have got rid of the Christian God, and now feel obliged to cling all the more firmly to Christian morality...With us it is different. When one gives up Christian belief one thereby deprives oneself of the *right* to Christian morality. For the latter is absolutely *not* self-evident...Christianity is a system, a consistently thought out and *complete* view of things. If one breaks out of it a fundamental idea, the belief in God, one thereby breaks the whole thing to pieces...Christianity presupposes that man does not know, *cannot* know what is good for him and what evil: he believes in God, who alone knows. Christian morality is a command: its origin is transcendental...it possesses truth only if God is truth—it stands or falls with the belief in God.'[16] In brief, the existence of an understood and binding morality is conditional upon the belief that morality is metaphysical in origin, that there exists a 'moral world-order': if that belief goes, 'good and evil' becomes problematic, morality ceases to be a matter of instinct, and moral values thus lose the force which only an instinctive certitude of their validity can give them.

In Europe, the power of the moral instinct derives from the belief that moral commands are the will of God: the Christian dogma is that the will of God exists and is known; to do good is to act in accordance with God's will, to do evil is to act counter to God's will; the good will be rewarded ('saved'), the wicked punished ('damned'). This dogma lost its power, but the morality communicated by it outlasted it, though in a more mundane and 'human' shape. During the bourgeois age it assumed the form: what is right and wrong is fairly well known, intuitively, to everyone; if you do what you know to be right you will be happy, if you do what you know to be wrong you will be unhappy until you have returned to the path of rectitude; those who do right will somehow come out well in the last accounting, those who persist in wrongdoing will come out ill. I think this a fair summary of what constitutes bourgeois morality, and I think too that the events of our own age have shown how inadequate it is, and that Nietzsche was right when he maintained that it constitutes an unstable half-way stage between morality founded on belief in the known will of God (the existence of a 'moral world-order') and the disappearance of morality with the disappearance of this belief. 'Extreme positions are not succeeded by moderate ones,' he wrote, 'but by *contrary* extreme positions. And thus the belief in the absolute immorality of nature, in purpose- and meaning-lessness, is the psychologically necessary *affect* once belief in God and an essentially moral order can no longer be maintained.'[17]

If we recall now the names which summarize the tradition in which Mann placed himself, we shall find that two of them belong to men stigmatized by Nietzsche as exhibiting in a pre-eminent degree the *pathos* attending the moral nihilism just described. 'Pessimism [is] a preliminary form of nihilism',[18] he writes—pessimism understood as the feeling that, since life is not a moral phenomenon, it is morally valueless and therefore valueless altogether. This feeling compels to a condemnation of life because life is not moral and to a repudiation of it and of one's own life, negatively as a disgusted turning-away and withdrawal, positively as the desire for self-destruction. It was in *Schopenhauer* that Nietzsche—speaking, like Mann, in terms of the German tradition—saw this world-denying pathos first become clearly conscious and influential; and in *Wagner*, Schopenhauer's most famous disciple, he saw the great exemplar of what Schopenhauer had taught. We shall discover that these are precisely the roles assigned to Schopenhauer and Wagner in Thomas Mann's fiction.

5

The *pathos of nihilism*—the feeling that there is no truth and no morality, and that life might as well end as go on—became a public fact in Germany during the early years of the present century. Nietzsche had written that 'man would rather will *nothingness* than *not* will',[19] and that a people of strong will to power deprived of satisfaction will will its own destruction rather than refrain from the exercise of will; and that was what, by all appearances, it was coming to in Germany. The

Reich — the 'German Empire', which was not merely an area of land and its populace but an empire of the spirit — went down to moral and physical destruction unparalleled in the modern world because it *wanted to*, because there was nothing left for it but to want to. Throughout this century Germany has *wanted to be destroyed*.

This is the meaning of Hitler: a nation's secret will to perish made flesh: the nihilistic pathos incarnate. This is the meaning of the extremity of crime into which he led his followers: no affront to the old morality appeared bad enough to exhaust the passion for moral destruction until that moment when the genius of nihilism itself, the voice of nothingness, suggested to him a crime which would be the perfect mirror of its own motivation: the destruction of an entire race. For what makes the brain reel and the heart stop at contemplation of this crime is not so much the horror of the thing itself — for there have been many horrible crimes, and the terror and agony felt by one soul is not increased because there are six million others who feel it too — no, it is rather the apparent absurdity and meaninglessness of the whole endeavour. With what vigour it is carried out, and with what refinement of dreadfulness; with what expenditure of material needed elsewhere in the middle of a world war; and when the system which makes it possible is itself visibly doomed the enterprise is pushed forward with greater and greater zeal, as if its perpetrators are afraid they will be stopped before they have finished. What total upside-downness, what a somersault of values! But that precisely is its explanation, its meaning, that is the answer to the question Why? The great crime was a mirror of that which motivated it.

The idea of the physical extermination of the *Germans* seems never to have been far from Hitler's thoughts. At the beginning of the final stage of the war, when Germany was surrounded by enemies whom it had inoculated with an overwhelming hatred of everything German, he assured his people that the Allies were going to exert themselves 'to smash (*zerschlagen*) our *Reich* and to annihilate (*vernichten*) the German people and its social order. Their ultimate goal,' he went on, 'is the extermination of German man (*die Ausrottung des deutschen Menschen*)'.[20] But this is only a repetition of what, it appears, he had always believed: in the now famous 'secret memorandum' on the Four-Year Plan of 1936 — in which he decreed 'I. The German army must be ready for action within four years. II. The German economy must be on a war footing within four years' — he gives as the reason for this belligerency the necessity of defending Germany against Soviet Russia by attacking first. 'For,' he says, 'a victory of Bolshevism over Germany would lead, not to a Versailles Treaty, but to a conclusive annihilation (*Vernichtung*), indeed extermination (*Ausrottung*) of the German people.'[21] The language, like all Hitler's language, exposes the vacant depths of his soul: *zerschlagen, vernichten, Ausrottung*, the words in which the nihilistic pathos expresses itself most readily — destruction, extermination, annihilation, making into nothing — these words are forever on his lips, and what they express is the one thing about him which was not fraud: the urge for destruction which originates in the urge for *self*-destruction.

In face of this history- and mind-haunting deed — the annihilation of the Jews as a mirror-image of the annihilation of the Germans — the assembling of quotations seems a trivial affair. Let us none the less quote Nietzsche again: a passage in which the nature of one such as Hitler is reduced to the conceptual bones: 'Nihilism is not only a contemplation of the "in vain!" and not only the belief that everything deserves to perish: one sets to work, one *destroys*...It is a condition of strong minds and wills: and these do not find it possible to halt at the No of "judgment": — their nature demands the *No of the deed*. Reduction to nothing by judgment is seconded by reduction to nothing by hand.'[22] The clarity with which Hitler exhibits this destructive urge illuminates what preceded him. The first German war was entered upon in a mood altogether different from that of the drum-banging that went on in London and Paris: enthusiasm was founded as much on the possibility that Germany might be defeated and destroyed as on the possibility it might win. Mann caught that mood when he wrote that the German poets greeted war 'with deep-throated triumph — as though they and the nation could meet with nothing better, more beautiful, more fortunate, than that a desperately overwhelming enmity should rise against the nation'.[23] There can be no doubt about it: very many Germans wanted war — not victory (although they might have wanted that too) but *war*. They wanted to risk destruction. Destruction failed to come, but many continued to yearn for it.

The most famous expression of that yearning was Spengler's *The Decline of the West* (*Untergang* is a rather stronger term than 'decline': 'The Going-Under of the West'). The arguments of that book are fanciful and worthless: what is interesting about them is that the author *wants* them to be valid: he wants the West to 'go under'. One could cite a regiment of others who in 1918 had not had enough of destruction; I shall limit myself to one who expressed himself with uncommon clarity: Moeller van den Bruch, an author whose crackbrained political ideas did not prevent him from being prophetic: 'For all peoples,' he wrote, 'comes the hour when they must die by murder or suicide, and no greater ending can be imagined for a people than destruction in a world war in which the whole earth had to rise and suppress a single country.'[24] Here is the nihilistic pathos pure: he wants annihilation. And when Hitler offered such men *Weltmacht oder Niedergang* he offered both alternatives as being equally attractive, but with *Niedergang* as perhaps the more attractive of the two.

6

We seem to have got a long way away from the novels and stories of Dr Thomas Mann—but that is an illusion produced by the darkness of this uncanny region. We are in fact very close to them: we are *beneath* them, they are just above our heads. The German tradition turned upon itself; the disappearance of the metaphysical world and with it the sense that life is real and meaningful; the decay of moral values, the consequent confusion of good and evil, and the pathos arising from this confusion: these constitute the hollow earth upon which his fiction stands. It says a lot for his skill as a builder that he was able to erect such large structures and keep them standing on such shaking and shifting soil.

2 Ideology

I

Mann was born in 1875, in Lübeck in North Germany. His family was a family of merchants and senators of the kind described in *Buddenbrooks* and *The Magic Mountain*. His father was an old-style German conservative, his mother a musician of mixed German and Portuguese West African descent, and he exploited in his fiction the temperamental opposition between these two contrasted types. When he was 19 he left his native environment and went to live in Munich, the representative city of South Germany; subsequently he went further south, to Italy, where, while living with his elder brother, the novelist Heinrich Mann, he himself became a novelist and wrote his first novel, *Buddenbrooks*. He had already published a number of stories, but *Buddenbrooks* was an achievement of an altogether superior kind and its publication in 1901 made him into a leading German writer at the age of 25. He returned to Munich and lived as a writer and man of letters.

During this era of this life his explicit political opinions were conservative and nationalist. He welcomed the war because it would mean the end of the corrupting ease of peace: 'Germany's whole virtue and beauty', he wrote, 'is unfolded only in war.'[1] Thirty years later he narrated through the mouth of Serenus Zeitblom what sounds like a successful attempt to recall his feelings in 1914: 'War had broken out... In the guise of a disciplined execution of all the plans previously made and rehearsed, it raged through our cities and towns, as terror and exaltation, as the inevitable, as "destiny", as awareness of power and readiness for sacrifice, in the heads and hearts of men...its effect was undeniably and pre-eminently enthusiasm...I would by no means deny that I fully shared in the popular exultation, though its more extravagant ebullitions were foreign to my nature. My conscience...was not perfectly clear. Such a "mobilization" for war, however grim and stern a face it wears, must always have something about it like an unlicensed holiday...it seems a little like playing truant, like running away, like yielding to un-bridled instinct.'[2] Perhaps this has been a little coloured by the mellowing years, yet it seems to reflect the mingled enthusiasm and reservations which prompted the earlier of the wartime essays collected in 1918 as *Betrachtungen eines Unpolitischen*—a title which may have been suggested by Nietzsche's *Unzeit-gemässe Betrachtungen*. Certainly his enthusiasm for the war was very much modified by the events of the war itself, and the *Reflections of a Non-Political Man* move towards something like a repudiation of many of his former views.

His lecture of 1922 *On the German Republic* shows him to be approaching a 'Western democratic' outlook: he supports the Weimar Republic but does so, he says, because he sees it as a continuation of the German way of life. The appearance of *The Magic Mountain* in 1924 gave many the impression he had be-come a 'democrat', and by the end of the 1920s he had definitely acquired that reputation. Attacks on him by the Nazis were frequent, and when they came to power he was instantly denounced as a 'liberal-reactionary': he responded to the new regime by resigning from the Prussian Academy of Arts. From 1933 to 1939 he lived in Switzerland, and when, in 1936, he was deprived of his honorary doctorate at Bonn, he wrote in reply: 'The meaning and goal of the National Socialist state system is and can only be this: through the inexorable elimination, repression and extermination of every troublesome opposition to get the German people into shape for the "coming war" ':[3] which shows that his attitude towards a 'German war' had by then completely altered.

He had begun his *Joseph* novel before the Nazi accession, but the decision to bring the first part out in Berlin during 1933 should probably be understood as a political act. It was cer-tainly seen in that light by the writer Herbert Blank, who was then employed as a censor of literature, and remarked in his report on *The Tales of Jacob* that 'it is simply not endurable that, ten months after 30 January [the day Hitler became Chan-cellor], the emigrant Thomas Mann is able to retail in Germany a book full of Jewish tales'.[4] (The second part, *Young Joseph*, appeared in Berlin in the following year, but *Joseph in Egypt* had to be published in Vienna (1936) and *Joseph the Provider* in Stockholm (1943).)

Mann went to the United States in 1939 and in 1944 became

23

an American citizen. He broadcast to Germany both before and during the second war, and his conscious attitude towards Nazism may be summed up in his words: 'Hitler had the great merit of producing a simplification of the emotions, of calling forth a wholly unequivocal No.'[5] After the war he returned to Switzerland. Later he was the only prominent exile to be welcomed back by both East and West Germany: his political outlook had now become: 'Every reasonable human being should be a moderate Socialist.'[6] When he died in 1955 he was the one major writer admired equally by the Western world and the Communists. (Lukács is a good example of a Communist critic whose admiration for Mann is almost uncritical.)

Let us now see to what extent this ideological evolution is borne out and to what extent contradicted by the novels and stories: let us see whether all was as simple and direct as it appeared to be on the conscious surface.

2

Buddenbrooks is probably Mann's most widely-read novel; it is certainly the easiest to read. Its plot is usually summarized as the description of a family like his own and of its decline through four generations as business acumen gives place to artistic sensibility. This theme is, of course, present and very prominent; it is one of the novel's most important themes, as we shall later see; but there is another equally important: the decline of the Buddenbrooks coincides with the rise of the Hagenströms. If the Buddenbrook family is old Europe—and it is pretty clear that that is what the Buddenbrooks do represent —then the Hagenström family is that which displaced and succeeded old Europe, namely new Europe, the Europe of the twentieth century. But the Hagenströms represent nothing but primitive acquisitiveness. That they have no culture worth speaking of, that by comparison with the Buddenbrooks they are very vulgar and commonplace, is perhaps no more than colouring, something laid on to render them as unattractive as possible: the vital distinction, that which would remain if all the accidental or surface distinctions were removed (and will remain when, through the agency of wealth, security and position, they *are* removed) is the absence of *morality*. That which made the Buddenbrooks something more than brigands, the moral element, is lacking in the Hagenströms. The non-moral Hagenströms defeat the moral Buddenbrooks, and do so easily and quickly. How quickly is obscured by the habit of thinking of the novel as covering four generations, although its time-span is not nearly so great as that description suggests. Tony Buddenbrook is present on the first page as a girl of eight and on the last as an elderly lady: the decline of the family takes, in fact, just one lifetime. And the reason this family is so vulnerable is precisely the most obvious fact about it: that it is the model bourgeois family and its morality that transitional form which constitutes an unstable halfway stage between morality founded on belief in the known will of God and the disappearance of all morality with the disappearance of this belief. The future belongs to the Hagenströms because they already embody that morality of the future which is no morality at all.

The *instability* of bourgeois morality—the difficulty it experiences in standing upright and its consequent disposition to fall over when pushed—is insisted on again and again in *Buddenbrooks*. The central point of this morality—at once its symbol and the actual point at which moral behaviour is of the greatest practical necessity—is honest dealing over money. Dishonesty over money is, in the Buddenbrooks' world, dishonesty *per se*. What does the author tell us about the attitude of this world towards such dishonesty? A certain Weinschenk has been detected in what the law insists on regarding as a financial swindle, and has gone to prison; but 'this man had in all probability done no more than his business colleagues did every day and thought nothing of; if he had not been caught he would have gone his way with head erect and conscience clear...His testimony before the court had been given with the most sincere conviction; and people who understood the technicalities of the case supported his contention that he had merely executed a bold manoeuvre for the credit of his firm and himself—a manoeuvre known in the business world as usance.'[7] A little later the 'people who understood the technicalities of the case' discuss a similar case and reveal the moral uncertainty concealed behind such a term as 'usance': 'They began to talk about the latest town scandal—about P. Philipp Kassbaum, who had been falsifying bills of exchange

25

and now sat behind locks and bars. No one felt outraged over the dishonesty: they spoke of it as an act of folly, laughed a bit, and shrugged their shoulders.'[8]

It might be thought that these people — the Weinschenks and Kassbaums and the people who talk about them and share their outlook — are of the Hagenström persuasion and provide no evidence that the moral convictions of the genuine old-style bourgeois were in any way shaky or unsound. That this is not necessarily the case is evidenced by the fact that the Buddenbrooks, the model bourgeois, are themselves infected with a tendency to dishonesty over money.

The case is made, gradually but at last unmistakably, that the acquisition and preservation of money is for the Buddenbrooks the ultimate purpose of existence, that the family's tradition of 'loyalty to the firm' means in practice setting aside everything that hinders the acquisition and preservation of money, and that this 'everything' includes, if need be, that bourgeois morality whose central point is honesty over money. The fact is crucial for an understanding of this family and, indeed, for an understanding of the whole book and of Thomas Mann's attitude towards bourgeois morality. The ideology of 'loyalty to the firm' is so inimical to the true happiness of the Buddenbrooks that, although it seems to the most upright and strong-willed of them the very backbone of the family tradition, it is on the contrary and in reality a kind of ancestral curse which helps to ruin the lives and decompose the souls of the entire tribe: the lives and souls of those members of it who adhere to that ideology and of those who do not.

The effects of this curse are perceptible throughout the book. Jean, the father of Thomas, Christian and Tony, sacrifices his daughter's happiness to the acquisition of money by morally compelling her to marry Grünlich. That Grünlich turns out to be a swindler is not only the first grand instance of an honest exterior concealing corruption within and a hint that bourgeois rectitude may in general be none too certain (a hint more than borne out by the affair of Weinschenk), but also a poetic punishment of both Jean and Tony, in as much as Tony preeminently shares her father's ideology of 'loyalty to the firm'. Tony goes on to a succession of unfortunate marriages, all of them a direct consequence of this loyalty and of that original betrayal of life for the sake of the Buddenbrook fortune which she perpetrated when she abandoned Morton Schwarzkopf, with whom she was in love, in order to marry Grünlich, whom she disliked. It may be noted that the memory of this original act of betrayal, and of the possibilities of natural happiness which its commission annihilated, lingers on in her subconscious mind throughout her life: its presence is revealed by her uttering, on the most diverse occasions, Schwarzkopf's unorthodox opinions in the very words in which he had long ago uttered them to her. Thomas, the central figure of the book and the embodiment of the Buddenbrook ideology, naturally falls most heavily under the curse, and we shall later see it working upon him in other connexions; here it will suffice to say that the scene in which he has his only serious quarrel with his mother is the book's most unambiguous declaration of the deleterious effect of that ideology. 'What was going on? Something amazing, something dreadful, something at which the very actors in the scene themselves stood aghast and incredulous. A quarrel, an embittered disagreement between mother and son!' What is this unprecedented quarrel about? 'One hundred and twenty-seven thousand five hundred marks current' which the Frau Consul has given away to the fortune-hunting pastor Tiburtius.[9]

As for those who find they cannot share the family ideology, it is enough to point out that their lives are made difficult and they are on occasion virtually persecuted precisely because they cannot share it: Christian and Uncle Gotthold, for example, are regarded by the others almost as criminals, and despised as drop-outs, solely because they are by temperament incapable of subordinating everything in their lives to 'loyalty to the firm'.

But this is not the worst: that obsession with acquiring and preserving money — the curse of the Buddenbrooks — is precisely the agency through which the instability of that bourgeois morality which the Buddenbrooks represent is first made palpably evident. If the morality in which they believe happens to stand in the way of acquiring or preserving money, then the Buddenbrooks are capable of shutting their minds to it and acting dishonestly: and in that they are capable of doing so they reveal themselves as being *potentially* what the Hagenströms are *actually* — and reveal too why the latter experience so little difficulty in displacing them: they stand to the Buddenbrooks in the relation of actual to potential. The scene in which the speck of decay is first disclosed in the Buddenbrooks' moral core is worth reproducing in detail: it shows the skill and subtlety with which Mann goes to work on this theme.

Jean is discussing with Grünlich the amount of Tony's dowry: ' "I entirely agree with you, my good friend. This important matter must be settled. In short, then: the usual dowry of a young girl of our family is seventy thousand marks." Herr Grünlich cast at his future father-in-law a shrewd, calculating glance—the glance of the genuine man of business. [At this 'genuine man of business' we should remember that Grünlich is a conscious and calculating swindler.] "You know, my honoured father," he began again, "the deep respect I have for traditions and principles. Only—in the present case is not this consideration for the tradition a little exaggerated? A business increases— a family prospers—in short, conditions change and improve." "My good friend," said the Consul, "you see in me a fair-dealing merchant. You have not let me finish, or you would have heard that I am ready and willing to meet you in the circumstances, and add ten thousand marks to the seventy thousand without more ado." "Eighty thousand, then," said Herr Grünlich, making motions with his mouth, as though to say: "Not *too* much; but it will do." Thus they came to an affectionate settlement; the Consul jingled his keys like a man satisfied as he got up. And, in fact, his satisfaction was justified; for it was only with the eighty thousand marks that they had arrived at the dowry traditional in the family.'[10]

Thus the 'fair-dealing merchant'. A little thing in itself, perhaps, but big in implication: Jean's morality is such that it permits him to start what is supposed to be a lifelong relationship with Grünlich by lying to him about and swindling him over money.

Although the Hagenströms and their kind are certainly 'bourgeois' in the accepted meaning of the word, they cannot be bourgeois in the sense in which Mann uses it in the title of his essay *Goethe as Representative of the Bourgeois Age*. The 'bourgeois age' is the age of the defeated Buddenbrooks and therefore lies in the past. The new age, bourgeois in name but something else in spirit, is the property of the victorious Hagenströms, the representatives of a new barbarism characterized by the absence of any moral imperative. That, in its aspect as social criticism, is the conclusion of *Buddenbrooks*.

3

The ideological implications of *The Magic Mountain* are more complex—for Mann had by the date of this novel come to love complexity for its own sake. The key figures are Settembrini and Naphta: the former is usually taken to be the advocate of humanism and democracy, the latter that of obscurantism and reaction, and the author is assumed to be, with whatever reservations, on the side of Settembrini. This view is not *altogether* wrong: what is wrong with it is that it trivializes these two figures and thus obscures Mann's actual attitude towards them, while failing to perceive their connexion with the climactic episode of the book, the vision in the sub-chapter 'Snow'. What we shall need to do, as briefly as may be, is to abstract from the wealth of detail lavished upon Settembrini and Naphta their essential attributes and thus understand *who they are*: once this is understood, the rest will follow.

Settembrini appears first. In his odd and worn-out clothing, in the fact that he always wears it and is never seen in any other, and in his habit of supporting himself on his cane as he stands and addresses the world, he is Chaplinesque, he has something of the clown and figure of comedy about him from the first. It is as a consequence of this rather than of anything he says that the reader sides with him: undoubtedly he is one of the most sympathetic figures in all Mann's work (although this is perhaps not saying very much). From the beginning he shows himself to be almost ridiculously well-read: he is a compendium of the humanities, and quotes from all the major European literatures. His credo is enlightenment, rationality, humanism, a concatenation of beliefs which he sums up in the one word 'civilization'![11] But that this credo is not altogether pure, that there is something cracked about it (or at least about Settembrini himself) is revealed very early on, when a long tirade on the coming 'universal brotherhood of man' and on the conflict between 'force and justice, tyranny and freedom, superstition and knowledge' culminates in a demand that 'Austria must be crushed, crushed and dismembered'.[12] 'Hans Castorp did not care for this last drift' in Settembrini's argument,[13] and his dubiety proves well founded when it later appears that Settembrini's liberalism involves him in being, not only violently anti-Austrian, but also violently anti-Russian: 'Wolves of the steppes, snow, vodka, the knout, Schlüsselburg, Holy Russia'[14] is more of a bugbear to him even than Austria: both are, in his judgment, 'Asiatic', and his reference to Genghis Khan in connexion with Russia reveals that his basic feeling towards both these states is one of fear. Is that possibly also the origin of his entire credo of 'universal brotherhood'? Does his commitment to rationality and enlightenment originate in fear of their opposites, that is to say in a *reactive* emotion, so that his apparently firm and positive intellectual position would in reality rest on literally trembling foundations?

I would regard some such suspicion, or at least the suspicion that this intellectual position of his is not to be taken absolutely at face value, as receiving confirmation in the course of the long dialogue with Castorp during which Settembrini produces from 'the baggy side pocket of his pilot coat' a bundle of papers from the 'International League for the Organization of Progress' and goes on to outline an impossibly literal 'comprehensive and scientifically executed programme...embracing all the projects for human improvement conceivable at the moment'.[15] The objective of the league he proclaims to be 'combating human suffering by the available social methods, to the end of finally eliminating it altogether', and this objective is to be pursued by 'the publication of a series of volumes bearing the general title: *The Sociology of Suffering*. It should be the aim of the series', he proceeds, 'to classify human suffering according to classes and categories, and to treat it systematically and exhaustively.'[16] The league for the organization of progress and the elimination of human suffering I take to be a *reductio ad absurdum* of liberal enlightenment, and the seriousness with which Settembrini takes it a sign that he has now passed over frankly into caricature and farce. What is contradictory and laughable in his nature is henceforward emphasized and exposed to the limelight: on one occasion it is said of him that his manner of speaking when he is trying to entrap the inquisitorial Naphta itself 'had something in it of the inquisitor waiting to pounce upon the witness so soon as he shall have involved himself in an admission of guilt';[17] on another, that he 'enjoined him [Naphta] to be calm—his own voice shaking with passion'.[18]

Settembrini's self-confidence is immense, and until Naphta appears he seems to possess exclusive tenancy of the ear of Hans Castorp, whom he is seeking to convince. But although

Hans—who, as representative of the common man, is not very articulate—puts up little intellectual resistance to Settembrini's arguments, his mind is already turned to listen to the voice of Naphta even before that obscurantist has been heard of. We know from the author's and from his own account that he has always 'taken an interest in mournful and edifying things',[19] and it is this *penchant* for the dark and mysterious which in the first instance constitutes his strongest barrier of resistance to Settembrini's gospel of luminous lucidity. But this barrier is as nothing compared with another which comes to be paradoxically identified with it: his passion for Madame Chauchat. In the dialectical scheme of the novel, Clavdia Chauchat is the bodily objectivization of that of which Naphta is the voice. That she is Russian and looks 'Tartar', that she announces her appearance by the uncivilized act of letting the door of the dining hall slam behind her, is the merest beginning of her role as antithesis to Settembrini's 'civilization'. When Hans has become 'over head and ears in love' with her he recognizes quite clearly that in this condition one loses interest in the civilization of a Settembrini, that one is 'simply not at home to pedagogic influences, however republican, however eloquent', and experiments with minor acts of uncivilized behaviour, including letting the door of the dining hall slam behind him, which acts he finds 'both fitting and agreeable'.[20] He discovers too that moral judgment has 'nothing to do'[21] with being in love, and that 'when one is in love, the aesthetic judgment counts for as little as the moral'.[22] The Walpurgis Night carnival has the function, among other functions, of taking him away from Settembrini and all that he represents over to the side of Madame Chauchat and all that *she* now represents: away from that 'civilization' whose light is ineffective to pierce the Walpurgis Night gloom, over to that state in which moral and aesthetic judgments are in suspense and one deliberately flouts 'the accepted form employed in the educated countries of the West' and insists on calling everyone 'du'. By midsummer we discover him exalting over the way in which our 'rude forefathers' used to celebrate 'the very midday and zenith of the year' and asking whether the reason for their rejoicing was not that 'from then on the world went down into the dark...Tragic joy, triumphant sadness,' he exclaims, '—that was what made our ancestors leap and exult around the leaping flames: they

31

did so as an act of homage to the madness of the circle, to an eternity without duration, in which everything recurs—in sheer despair, if you like.'[23] Having reached the point of quoting Nietzsche, he is now in a fit state to hear the voice of the dialectical antithesis to Settembrini's rationalistic daylight in addition to feeling its power: from Madame Chauchat he goes on to the conscious advocate of the dark, Leo Naphta. (This, by the way, is the reason Madame Chauchat thereafter plays a minor role, a fact I have heard advanced as an objection to the novel and a criticism of the novelist.)

In reflecting on Naphta, let us note first of all that he sometimes voices opinions which Hans Castorp has held all along. Consider (since the subject will be of interest to us later on) the question of the relation of genius to disease. 'Herr Settembrini had progress ever on his lips', Naphta is reported as saying: 'was he aware that all progress, in so far as there was such a thing, was due to illness, and to illness alone? In other words, to genius, which was the same thing? Had not the normal, since time was, lived on the achievements of the abnormal?'[24] (It is worth remarking now that, in *Doctor Faustus*, the Devil tells Adrian Leverkühn precisely the same thing.[25]) But Hans has long previously given voice to a sentiment very similar to this: 'One always has the idea of a stupid man as perfectly healthy and ordinary, and of illness making one refined and clever and unusual. At least as a rule—.' Settembrini's reaction to these words was emphatically to deny their truth—'my position is one of absolute dissent'—and to go on to apply to them the worst epithet in his vocabulary: 'superstition'.[26] In this important matter, then, Hans had been for Naphta and against Settembrini from the beginning.

As the antithesis to Settembrini, Naphta is always well-dressed, and where his appearance deviates from the normal it is in the direction of the sinister rather than that of the clownish. He is very ugly and in sundry other respects unpleasing and repellent. In warning Hans against him, Settembrini characterizes him 'with a single word. He is a voluptuary',[27] and adds that 'all his thoughts are voluptuous and stand under the aegis of death'.[28] This description can hardly be considered disinterested, but seems none the less to be borne out by the account of Naphta's life, where it is said that, as a consequence of his early experiences, 'the conception of piety came to be bound up in his mind with that of cruelty, and the idea of the sacred and the spiritual with the sight and smell of spurting blood',[29] and his world is compared with that of a soldier in their common 'attitude towards the shedding of blood'.[30] Hans himself describes him as a 'reactionary revolutionist': I have no doubt the only reason he does not employ the word 'fascist' is that it had not then been invented. He is in his way almost as well-read as Settembrini and almost as much of a compendium —in this case, of esoteric and ecclesiastical literature. His credo is not so easy to summarize in a few words as Settembrini's, except perhaps as a negation of that: unenlightenment, irrationality, anti-humanism: 'your humanity is today nothing but a tail end', he informs Settembrini, '...it is yawning its head off, while the new Revolution, *our* Revolution, my dear sir, is coming on apace to give it its quietus. We, when we sow the seeds of doubt deeper than the most up-to-date and modish free-thought has ever dreamed of doing, we well know what we are about. Only out of radical scepsis, out of moral chaos, can the Absolute spring, the anointed Terror of which the time has need.'[31] His demand for the undoing of the Enlightenment, and his advocacy of a Terror which will abolish the modern world and restore what Settembrini would call the Dark Ages, do not lend themselves so easily to parody as do Settembrini's proposals for the organization of progress: but this concatenation of ideas is quite often taken to the limit of the credible and passes into self-caricature of a sort—as, for example, when Naphta is made to advocate illiteracy.[32]

Many pages of the novel are covered by the debates which these two opposite types conduct together, with Hans Castorp as the audience they are supposedly trying to convince. Now, if these debates are read as philosophical discussions, the outcome will be that, like Hans Castorp, the reader will reject both disputants as muddle-heads, and go on to damn the author as a mentally befogged Teuton. As philosophy, the debates between Settembrini and Naphta are simply a waste of time, a welter of confusion, and any criticism of *The Magic Mountain* founded on the idea that they *are* philosophical debates, which ought to reach some tenable conclusion but do not, is itself confused. When Naphta and Settembrini talk together they do not *debate* at all; no logical argumentation occurs; neither is *ever* convinced by something the other has said; and no statement ever follows logically from another: in short, there is no more *philosophy* in them than there is in an argument between the wind and the side of a house. One of them stands, the other buffets and batters against him. But what, if they are not philosophical discussions, is the purpose of these confrontations? Their purpose is the exposition, in as many differing contexts as the author has the knowledge to employ, of the antagonism between what the two men represent, namely the cold light of rationality and the dark world of will and desire. These two forces do not 'debate'—they merely come into conflict.

This conflict is made somewhat obscure by the endeavour above mentioned to exhibit it over as wide an area as possible, with the result that the text is excessively crowded with assertions of fact and opinion drawn from a vast range of topics, and each of the two contestants is compelled to serve as the vehicle for a large assortment of qualities: Naphta, for example, has to be both Jew and Jesuit, Settembrini both freethinker and Freemason. But if we try to see through this dense characterization down to the essential being of each of them, we shall find (and not be surprised to find) that Settembrini is somewhat divorced and removed from the real world of passion and error, while Naphta often gives voice to it with uncommon bluntness and disdain for euphemism—that Settembrini seems to live on the face of the magic mountain, while Naphta has as it were an ear for the sounds coming from within it.

Settembrini declares that 'our Western heritage is reason—reason, analysis, action, progress':[33] Naphta knows better than that and takes great pleasure in his knowledge. Settembrini reproaches him with seeing 'nothing but political trickery in the lofty exertions of democracy to fufil itself internationally', to which Naphta retorts that what he *does* see 'is the last feeble stirrings of the instinct of self-preservation, the last remnant at the command of a condemned world-system. The catastrophe', he adds, 'will and must come.'[34] These exchanges occur during their first confrontation, which Settembrini breaks off with a characteristic remark expressing his normal unwillingness to recognize that a point of view differing from his own can possibly be genuine: 'You are joking of course—you can't mean what you say.'[35] Castorp's summary of it afterwards is 'What a mix-up!'[36] and one can sympathize: yet he thinks it a mix-up only because he thinks he has been listening-in on a meeting of the local debating society. That this is not the case is evidenced by the terms in which the disputants renew their conflict later on. After Settembrini has delivered a thunderous oration on 'pure knowledge...science...the unfettered quest for truth', Naphta responds 'with disagreeable composure' that 'there is no such thing as pure knowledge', that 'pure science is a myth'; when Settembrini returns to the attack by asking him whether he believes 'in truth, in objective, scientific truth, to strive after the attainment of which is the highest law of all morality', he replies that truth is 'whatever profits a man...He is the measure of all things, and his welfare is the sole and single criterion of truth.'[37] These exchanges, and hundreds more of the same sort, are reiterations of the undeviating antagonism between them: they are not 'discussion'.

This antagonism and antithesis continues unchanged and undiminished until the end, where it receives its most emphatic statement in the differing degree to which the two are aware of the approach of war: Settembrini's awareness is late, hesitant, and founded entirely on his knowledge of the transient political line-up of the time, Naphta's is early and as it were *seismic* — he *feels* the war coming.[38] In their final, fatal encounter — proposed, of course, by Naphta — although both are willing to die, Settembrini can only think of offering himself passively to be shot, while Naphta takes the active step of shooting himself.

Now, if we cast our mind over their confrontations as a whole, we shall receive the general impression that Naphta is unsympathetic, vehement, cynical, provocative, and, in the light of the actual course of European history, *right*: and that Settembrini is sympathetic, idealistic, angry only when provoked, and, in the light of the actual course of European history, *wrong*. But this conclusion will not cause us any surprise if we recall our earlier, hesitant conclusion that Settembrini's credo of rationality and humanism might have originated in fear of its opposite — in fear, that is, of Naphta: so that Naphta would represent 'truth' and Settembrini an attempt to negate 'truth', to substitute something else, something more comfortable and reassuring, in place of 'truth'. If that were the case, Naphta would be the original, positive force, and Settembrini the derivative, reactive force. That is, indeed, the relative positions occupied by will and reason in the philosophy of Schopenhauer, in which will is primary, reason secondary. But the pathos is wrong: Settembrini is not so much 'reason' as 'rationality', a late-erected and still unstable *barrier* against the forces of destruction and darkness. And at this point we are compelled, as Hans Castorp was and as Thomas Mann seems to have been, to resort again to Nietzsche.

Hans's vision in 'Snow' involves a scene in which a beautiful and happy race who resemble idealized Athenians live and enjoy life around a temple within the deepest recesses of which unspeakable horrors are being perpetrated. The moral of this vision is stated in the italicized sentence: '*For the sake of goodness and love, man shall let death have no sovereignty over his thoughts.*'[39] As Ronald Gray has pointed out, the details of the vision derive from the last paragraph of Nietzsche's *The Birth of Tragedy*: 'That this effect [the Apollonian 'transfiguration' of the 'Dionysian basic ground of the world'] is necessary anyone would appreciate most assuredly by intuition if he had ever felt, even if only in a dream, that he was carried back into the life of ancient Greece: walking among lofty Ionic colonnades, looking up towards a horizon cut off by clean and noble lines, beside him reflections of his transfigured form in shining marble, all around him solemnly pacing or delicately moving human beings speaking in harmonious sounds and rhythmic gestures — with this constant influx of beauty, would he not have to exclaim, raising his hand to Apollo: "Blessed people of Hellas! How great must Dionysus be among you if the god of Delos considers such magic necessary to heal your dithyrambic madness!" — To one so affected, however, an old Athenian, looking up at him with the sublime eyes of Aeschylus, might reply: "But say this, too, curious stranger: how much did this people have to suffer to be able to become so beautiful! But now follow me to the tragedy and sacrifice with me in the temple of both divinities!" '[40] I think anyone who reads Hans's vision will recognize that it originates in this passage; so that it will seem at any rate possible that if we have grasped the meaning of this passage we shall be on the way to grasping the meaning of the vision and of its italicized moral.

Nietzsche's intention in *The Birth of Tragedy* (his first book) was to explain the origin of art in the imposition of form and measure (Apollo) upon the primitive emotions (Dionysus): the outcome is a species of 'illusion' masking the terrible face of reality. If the power of Dionysus over a people is very great —

36

if, that is to say, they are a ferocious and barbaric people, as Nietzsche asserted the primitive Greeks were—then, if they succeed in controlling him, the result will be an art and culture of a very high and beautiful order, since the Apollonian form-giving force will have to have been even more powerful among this people than Dionysus. The closing image of the book is that of a visitor to the Greek world declaring the obviousness of this fact, and then being reminded by Aeschylus that the message of tragedy is that both gods, Dionysus and Apollo, are required for the production of this civilized beauty. This is the picture reproduced in Hans Castorp's vision amid the Alpine snow. But the moral Hans draws from it proceeds, not from the picture directly, but from reflecting and meditating on it: and these reflections take us further forward in *The Birth of Tragedy*—forward to those passages in which Nietzsche asserts that, as Greek tragedy was born when Aeschylus and Sophocles embodied Dionysus in Apollonian form, so it was killed when Euripides tried to eliminate 'that original and all-powerful Dionysian element' and to construct tragedy anew 'on the basis of un-Dionysian art, custom and philosophy'.[41] The consequence of this endeavour was the birth of a new antithesis: in place of Apollo and Dionysus 'the Dionysian and the Socratic'; henceforth Socratic optimism is set against Dionysian pessimism, and philosophy takes the place of art. The 'supreme law' of 'aesthetic Socratism' is that 'what is to be called beautiful must also be rational'.[42] Socrates is subsequently described as 'the specific *non-mystic*'[43] and as 'the type of the *theoretical man*' who was able, not only to live, but to die 'under the guidance of the scientific instinct'.[44] I suggest that the moral Hans draws from reflecting on his vision is therefore not that both gods—the sublime and the terrible—must be worshipped equally, but that, in the service of the one, the other must be *put down*: for the sake of goodness and love, man shall let death have no sovereignty over his thoughts.

All this might lead one to think that Settembrini is Socrates and Naphta Dionysus, and that Hans Castorp, adopting the position of Euripides, finally opts for Settembrini: but this conclusion is as a whole vitiated by the fact that Hans does *not* opt for Settembrini but persists in being unable to decide between the two opposite extremes up to the very end of the novel. That fact, however, ought not to disturb us very greatly provided we go even further forward in *The Birth of Tragedy*, forward, that is, to the beginning—to the 'Essay in Self-Criticism' prefaced by Nietzsche to the 1886 edition and printed in all subsequent editions. In this critical preface Nietzsche says that, as a consequence of his youthful enthusiasm, he had misunderstood the nature of his problem: he had been discussing the antithesis between the Socratic and the Dionysian in terms of *art*, whereas what he had really 'got hold of' then was 'the *problem of science* itself'.[45] What, he asks, 'is the meaning of all science? What is the end—or worse, what is the beginning —of all science? Is the spirit of science perhaps no more than fear in the face of pessimism and flight from it? A subtle means of self-defence against—the *truth*?'[46] Two years later, in *Twilight of the Idols*, he expanded this thought in a way very relevant to our discussion. He seeks, he says, 'to understand out of what idiosyncrasy that Socratic equation reason = virtue = happiness derives: that bizarrest of equations and one which has in particular all the instincts of the older Hellenes against it'.[47] His conclusion is that Socrates was in danger of being overwhelmed by his passions and therefore needed to assert the power of rationality to an exceptional degree: and he contends that Socrates became a public success because 'all the world had need of him...Everywhere the instincts were in anarchy; everywhere people were but five steps from excess..."The instincts want to play the tyrant; we must devise a *counter-tyrant* who is stronger"...If one needs to make a tyrant of *reason*, as Socrates did, then there must exist no little danger of something else playing the tyrant. Rationality...was *de rigueur*, it was their *last* expedient...one had only *one* choice: either to perish or—be *absurdly rational*...Reason = virtue = happiness means merely: one must imitate Socrates and counter the dark desires by producing a permanent *daylight*—the daylight of reason.'[48]

We have come a long way round—there was no other way round—but we have finally got home. Settembrini is the principle of rationality, of 'permanent *daylight*', as in Nietzsche's conception of Socrates; Naphta is 'the dark desires' as a counter to which this permanent daylight is produced. Settembrini is 'fear in the face of pessimism and flight from it, a subtle means of self-defence against—the *truth*'; Naphta is everything that Settembrini fears and defends himself against. And this is why, although Hans Castorp decides he will shut the voice of Naphta out of his mind, his creator will not let him, but makes him forget this resolve almost as soon as he has made it; why he continues to allow Settembrini to be wrong and Naphta right about the nature of life. In terms of Hans's vision, Settembrini is civilization, Naphta the horror which lies concealed behind it; and the voice of Naphta continues to compete successfully with the voice of civilization because his is the voice of reality and that of civilization that of a beautiful *illusion.*

Is Mann 'on the side of' Settembrini? But even to ask the question is an unbearable trivialization of the issues exposed in *The Magic Mountain.* Settembrini represents the ideals we have been brought up on and give our life meaning — but they are illusions, fear-inspired and truth-defying barriers against reality. That, in its aspect as social criticism, is the conclusion of *The Magic Mountain.*

4

Naphta and Settembrini are articulate to the point of resolving themselves entirely into words; Hans Castorp is only moderately articulate, he speaks hesitantly and without much self-assurance; but Mynheer Peeperkorn is for most of the time altogether inarticulate. He speaks in disjointed phrases and sudden exclamations. Yet when he does manage to get out a few connected sentences 'all interest in Settembrini's and Naphta's antinomies'[49] falls away and he is left total master of the field. Hans cannot finally side with either Settembrini or Naphta, but he falls instantly under the spell of Peeperkorn, and when Peeperkorn says he is willing to accept him as a brother, Hans declares himself 'so proud, so joyful, as I could never have dreamed it was possible for me to be'.[50] Madame Chauchat, so remote and so disdainful towards Hans, is merely Peeperkorn's casual mistress and servant. The novel makes no mystery of Peeperkorn's significance: he is the type of the founder of religions, the embodiment of the force of personality in all its unspeakable and therefore inarticulate power, which is stronger than the power of reason or the power of virtue. When, at his last public appearance, Peeperkorn's voice is rendered inaudible by the noise of the waterfall, so that those around him sit and listen, not to him, but to the roaring and thunder of the cataract, he becomes the embodiment of the most primitive of the religious feelings, the worship of nature and of the irresistible and all-subduing force of life itself.

Mynheer Peeperkorn dies in Haus Berghof, but in the mind of Thomas Mann he does not die, he lives on in unexpected forms. Later we shall see him reappear as 'the man of the blessing', the self-justifying personality and bearer of meaning, the incarnate victory over the nihilistic void; for the moment we must meet him in less attractive shape, that of the charismatic 'leader', an aspect of him associated with his lack of any clear 'ideas', with the fact that when he is not inarticulate or inaudible he merely describes natural events, such as the flight and swoop of an eagle, without commenting on them, so that the influence and attraction he exercises take place on a level below that of rationality and articulate speech and amount to a simple animal magnetism. Suppose this man — a man who dominates others by the force of his animal personality and by nothing else — transported down from the quasi-mythological heights of the magic mountain into the grubbiness of the real world, deprived of his eagle and waterfall, and made to walk the dusty streets: whom will he come to resemble? Will he not come to resemble the fake *cavaliere* Cipolla, *'forzatore, illusionista, prestidigitatore'*,[51] actually fairground hypnotist and, as is agreed on all hands, the living image of that other fairground hypnotist and *illusionista*, Mussolini?

(In parenthesis: the Dutchman Peeperkorn and the Italian Cipolla ('onion') both derive their names from the field of herbs and spices. It is an odd coincidence, though I presume no more than that, that when Brecht produced his version of Cipolla, his parody of the German version of Mussolini, he called him Ui, which is Dutch for 'onion'.)

Mynheer Peeperkorn's quality of animal magnetism, 'pure personality', is inherited by Cipolla in the form of the gift of hypnotism: the similarity between the two is obscured, not only by the difference in milieu, but more effectively by the conscious distaste Mann has come to feel for the charismatic 'personality' now it has begun to acquire actual followers, and followers of the baser sort, and to do so has had itself to put on a baser shape. It remains to be seen whether this distaste for the hypnotic leader transformed from Peeperkorn into Cipolla went very deep; whether Mann had entirely lost his appreciation of those powers, possessed by Peeperkorn and Cipolla alike, which are 'stronger than reason or virtue'.[52]

Mario and the Magician is taken to be an unambiguous exposure of fascism. The atmosphere of fascist Italy 'remains unpleasant in the memory' of the author and 'that dreadful being' Cipolla is the worst aspect of it.[53] The incident which leads to a change of hotel, the altercation on the beach which leads to a fine for injuring public morals, and the cowardice and bullying of the 'perfect terror' Fuggièro, are examples of the deterioration public behaviour has undergone since the rise of fascism. The author tells his children, who are with him and puzzled by the situation, that what is abroad is 'something rather like an illness, perhaps; not very pleasant, but probably unavoidable'.[54] The visit to Cipolla's evening of magic turns out to be the climax of the unpleasantness. The hall in which he is to perform stands at the proletarian end of the street in which it stands. All the town has gone down to see him, but he keeps them waiting until they begin to call out for him to appear, whereupon he appears at once. His costume is ill-fitting and he is at first laughed at 'from more than one quarter of the hall':[55] this laughter he treats with arrogant disdain, and by the exertion of his personal magnetism and the use of a riding-whip he is soon in command of the audience. The first demonstration of his powers — compelling a youth to stick out his tongue — involves characteristic vulgarity and incivility; and his numbers trick — conceptually simple though requiring considerable mental alertness to perform in practice — is only the preliminary to the real business of the evening, which is hypnotism. And then, until the very end of the performance — when, through an error of judgment, he gets himself shot by one of his victims — he has the assembled spectators at his mercy.

It will already have been noticed that he possesses certain characteristics in common with Mussolini, but there are others which make the correspondence more exact. It is said of him, for instance, that his 'persistent thin-skinnedness and animosity were in striking contrast to the self-confidence and worldly success he boasted of'; again, that 'so far, the man had done nothing; but what he had said was accepted as an achievement, by means of that he had made an impression';[56] again, that he 'had won his audience, though he by no means belonged to the class of men which the Italian...labels "*simpatico*"';[57] and again, that he repeatedly emphasizes the hardness of his lot as leader and mover of the audience, that he claims to suffer 'enormous hardship' in that role;[58] finally, that when he is confident he can do with the audience exactly what he likes 'there...crept into his voice a gross, autocratic note, and a kind of arrogance was in his sprawl'.[59]

We may accept that Cipolla is Mussolini, and in his role as fairground hypnotist he appears as repellent as ingenuity can make him. But there is another side to this picture. After a success with his card trick, the applauding audience 'conceded his possession of strange powers—strange whether for good or evil'.[60] When a young man made as if to attack him he 'kept quite cool and showed complete mastery of the situation' and exhibited 'calm superiority'.[61] It is said that 'everybody both enjoyed the amazing character of the entertainment and unanimously conceded the professional skill of the performer... it signified the triumph of objective judgment over antipathy and repressed resentment'.[62] It is said, again, that 'our feelings for Cavaliere Cipolla were of a very mixed kind...Were we under the sway of a fascination which emanated from this man...?'[63] And, again, that Cipolla was 'the most powerful hypnotist I have ever seen in my life'.[64]

One cannot fail to notice in these remarks a kind of admiration for Cipolla—a grudging admiration, if you will, but admiration none the less, signifying perhaps 'the triumph of objective judgment over antipathy and repressed resentment'. Indeed, I believe one cannot read the story without receiving the strong impression that Cipolla, his unpleasant qualities notwithstanding, is inordinately superior to everyone else in it. This superiority is made evident through his hypnotic powers, but it does not *consist* in these: they are an outward *sign* of an inner superiority, a superiority in respect of 'pure personality'. Is Mann himself conscious of this? In a sense he is, of course: he wrote the story and was capable of reading it afterwards and receiving the paramount impression it makes; and he also introduced a number of expressions of admiration for Cipolla into the text. But there is, none the less, throughout his long account of Cipolla's performance, an attempt to muddy and confuse our appreciation of his qualities as 'pure personality' by seeking to explain his powers in terms of 'will-power': and when we see that this explanation is faulty, we suspect that its purpose is to screen the author himself from the fascination exercised by the character.

The fullest version is given in connexion with Cipolla's greatest triumph, his success in compelling 'the gentleman from

Rome' (i.e. the Vatican) to dance against his will: 'If I understand what was going on, it was the negative character of the young man's fighting position which was his undoing. It is likely that *not* willing is not a practicable state of mind; *not* to want to do something may be in the long run a mental content impossible to subsist on. Between not willing a certain thing and not willing at all—in other words, yielding to another person's will—there may lie too small a space for the idea of freedom to squeeze into.'[65] Now, this explanation is confused, being both illogical in itself and untrue to the facts it seeks to explain. It is illogical because, if one is to admit the existence of the concept 'will' at all, 'not willing' will have to be simply its negation, the *absence* of will, and therefore 'not willing' cannot constitute a 'fighting position' or 'mental content', i.e. a *form* of will; it is untrue to the facts because the Roman gentleman is in fact 'willing' very hard, i.e. willing his legs and arms to stay still. These objections exist quite apart from the question whether one does in fact have any right to speak of 'will' at all, in connexion with hypnotism, or with the popular success of a fascist dictator, or in any other connexion.

This faulty explanation is the only one Mann attempts to account for Cipolla's hold over his audience; and since this is so, one is compelled to say that *Mario and the Magician,* far from being unambiguous, is characterized by illogicality of argument and ambivalence of feeling, and that the former is probably a consequence of the latter. Whatever the author's intentions, he has not been able to conceal that Cipolla (i.e. Mussolini, i.e. fascism) *did* exercise upon him a degree of fascination; and I suggest that anyone who doubts that should compare the effect of *Mario and the Magician* with that of Hemingway's *Che ti dice la patria*—a story whose theme is precisely the deterioration public behaviour had undergone in Italy since the rise of fascism, but which conveys unalloyed distaste for this deterioration and nothing else.

Where this fascination originates is not far to seek. On the one hand Cipolla is, as charismatic personality, another, if a somewhat debased and provincial, form of Mynheer Peeperkorn, before whose power Madame Chauchat and Hans Castorp bow down and worship and whose presence reduces to insignificance the polemics of Naphta and Settembrini; on the other he is, as fascist dictator, the spokesman of European nihilism in its political aspect — the public triumph of that morality of the future which is no morality whose rise Mann had described when he described the rise of the Hagenströms. The new barbarism which triumphed in *Buddenbrooks* has acquired a dynamic from the force of personality exhibited in *The Magic Mountain*. That, in its aspect as social criticism, is the conclusion of *Mario and the Magician*.

5

Thomas Mann is thorough. It is a national characteristic. The German version of Cipolla was a thousand times more thorough than his model and original — so much more thorough that his model seems to us today by comparison almost a friendly, familiar, old-style figure, or as a joke, a buffoon, a *buffo*. Mussolini was not without faults, but he remained human — and an Italian. Fascist Italy was life become grand opera: the plot was preposterous but the costumes were dazzling. When it was hit by reality it fell over, to be sure: it was only a stage-set. Italians are, alas, not thorough: they are too easily distracted and too easily pleased to be that. A little 'unreason', a little 'spitting on freedom', a little 'blood-bath' — that was enough, they were satisfied, they wanted something new: in the end — long before the end — they were *bored* with fascism. This life-loving and music-loving people had accepted as leader a man who was four-fifths operatic aria — but he kept repeating the same tune. And to be expected to fight and *die* for him! But nobody really dies in an opera!

How different was what took place on that other, Wagnerian stage. Wagnerian opera is *serious*. Wagner wanted the opera house to become a temple, a church: imagine that idea occurring to an Italian! (in Italy the churches are four-fifths opera house). On this stage the setting, the histrionics, the costumes, even the plot could be experienced religiously and mistaken for reality — they could *become* reality. No half-measures here! The hero, and before him the rest of the cast and chorus, have to die — in reality.

With the financial and vocal backing of the Hagenströms, the German Cipolla put on such a performance that he brought the house down: one might think — one *does* think if one thinks as I do — that, since that was the outcome of the performance, it might also have been its secret objective. As the house was falling,

Thomas Mann, driven out long before by the din and by disgust at some of the 'acts', wrote an account—a fearfully thorough account—of how it had all come to pass: *Doctor Faustus: The Life of the German Composer Adrian Leverkühn as Told by a Friend.*

This book is a monster: with the best will in the world one cannot love it. 'The great German novel', part melodrama, part collection of essays, part torture-chamber of language, *Doctor Faustus* is full of borrowings—so full I have come to suspect that it is only my ignorance which prevents me from recognizing the original of *every* incident in it. The book is *put together*, a product of the desk and the filing-cabinet. It is airless, horribly airless; it smells of the midnight, and worse of the *midday* lamp; one cannot breathe in it. The old Germany fails to live, it is only brought forth from a lumber room and it smells of must and mould. The worst result—I mean worst from a conventional point of view—is the way in which it cannot endure comparison with what it has borrowed: how Adrian's interview with the Devil cannot endure comparison with Ivan Karamazov's; how its borrowings from the Faust Book cannot endure comparison with the Faust Book itself. But one cannot, for reasons I shall give later, exclude the possibility that these effects were intentional—or at any rate that the pressure of his theme forced the author along just this path: the path of excessive borrowing, of degrading what has been borrowed, of lifeless characterization, and of everything else 'wrong' with *Doctor Faustus*. That it is a 'great' book, an enduring book; that it can justly take its place as the last of the four great monuments Mann erected to his existence—I do not doubt for a moment. It is faulty, to be sure, but it is part of the mystery of art that a work of art can be full of faults and yet worth ten thousand petty 'successes'.

There are signs in the text of *Doctor Faustus* that Mann would have liked to make the *political* implications of his novel simple and direct; but by this date—long before this date—he had become incapable of a simple and direct response to that which was moving towards its conclusion in Europe. If we did not already know something of the complexity of his mind, of its fundamental inability to give a univocal verdict on anything—or at least its inability to do so without having first voiced *other* verdicts, even *counter*-verdicts: if we did not already know that, we should find it very paradoxical that a work apparently intended as a forthright attack and condemnation should be so extremely complicated in structure. *Doctor Faustus* is famously a novel with four or five levels of meaning: a circumstance which would, even if these levels of meaning were totally integrated one with another, militate against any sort of simplicity, directness or forthrightness. But these four- and five-fold significances are *not* thus integrated, they are *put together*, laid one on top of another: is it surprising therefore that, instead of seconding and supporting one another, they are sometimes mutually contradictory? so that, far from being direct and forthright, the novel is thoroughly and fundamentally ambiguous?

The prime cause of this contradiction and confusion is, as is only proper, the Devil—the nihilistic principle, '*der Geist, der stets verneint*'—and the role he plays in *Doctor Faustus*.

On one level, Adrian Leverkühn, the central figure of the novel, is a German composer whose life and career is described by his friend Serenus Zeitblom; on another, he is Nietzsche, inasmuch as the course of his life and that of Nietzsche's are in general and in a very large number of details identical (but he also borrows events from the lives of others, e.g. Tchaikovsky and Hugo Wolf); on a third level, he is the legendary Faustus, who sold his soul to the Devil in exchange for superhuman powers and was at the last taken to Hell; and on the final level, he is Germany, the German people. Now Mann assures us that the fits of rather cold and mirthless laughter of which Leverkühn is sometimes the victim indicate the presence of the Devil. When he read the opening chapters of the novel to Franz Werfel, he says, Werfel was struck '—or shall I say premonitively disturbed?—by Adrian's *laughter*, in which he instantly recognized something uncanny, an element of religious diabolism. He asked about it again and again...In that laughter the Devil, as the secret hero of the book, is invisibly present',[66] as he is, Mann adds, in other symbols, such as the experiments with inorganic growths.

This is very confusing—quite apart from the question whether Thomas Mann joins with the author of *The Song of Bernadette* in believing in the existence of the Devil. I cannot say that the diabolical presence in Leverkühn's laughter is something that leaps to the eye: but if the Devil *is* intended to be present there, he is going to play the Devil with the 'levels of meaning'! Leverkühn's laughter belongs on level one, the literal level: it is a characteristic of the German composer Adrian Leverkühn.

It also belongs on level two, inasmuch as it recalls Nietzsche's exortations to laugh even when there is not very much to laugh about. The Devil, however, belongs only on level three, the Faust level: on levels one and two he does not exist. On the literal level the Devil is something imagined by Leverkühn after his brain has become infected by syphilis. Adrian believes, with Hans Castorp and Naphta, that genius and illness are the same thing, and in that conviction he deliberately infects himself. His subsequent dialogue with the Devil is, as in the parallel case of Ivan Karamazov, a monologue in which he speaks out to himself his own most secret thoughts. The rationale of this aspect of the novel is that the supernatural events of the Faust legend are in reality imaginings, they belong to the mind, and in the life of Leverkühn they are restored to the mind and are all the product of disease. So long as *Doctor Faustus* is faithful to this idea it is not involved in any ambiguity, but is on the contrary very solid work and very imaginative. But this is not nearly enough for Mann. He wants the fictional Leverkühn to represent, not only the legendary Faust, but also the *real* Germany: and this involves him in making Leverkühn the victim of *real* forces, that is forces outside his own mind, with the consequence that the Devil and other elements of the Faust legend are introduced into his biography (the literal level) as real events and in circumstances under which they cannot be merely a product of his mind. Is the Devil in *Doctor Faustus* a real personage, the 'secret hero of the book'? If he is, he can appear during Leverkühn's boyhood — disguised as mocking laughter, inorganic growths, the eccentrics of Kaisersaschern, or in any other disguise — and at any other time or place, and the sense of the novel is that Leverkühn-Faust has literally sold his soul and Germany has done literally the same thing: in this event, however, all those passages in the novel inspired by the idea of restoring the events of the Faust legend to the mind are fundamentally misleading as to the novel's meaning. If the Devil is not a real personage, he cannot appear during Leverkühn's boyhood or at any other time before Leverkühn is infected, nor can he embody himself in anything which is not a product of Leverkühn's imagination, and the sense of the novel is that Leverkühn-Faust has *symbolically* sold his soul and Germany has done symbolically the same thing: in *this* event, however, it is all those passages which suggest the independent existence of the Devil which are fundamentally misleading. The fact of the matter is that the Devil in *Doctor Faustus* is both an independent personage *and* the product of Adrian's diseased brain: which is as much as to say that his role in the novel is fundamentally ambiguous.

The ambiguity and contradictoriness of the 'secret' hero spreads its influence over the whole book, the reason being that one does not know whether the ostensible hero Leverkühn is to be regarded as the author of the catastrophe which strikes him or as merely its victim. If the Devil is a real personage, then Leverkühn (Nietzsche-Faust-Germany) is seduced and destroyed by a force stronger than he and is to be pitied; if the Devil is a figment of Leverkühn's imagination, then Leverkühn (Nietzsche-Faust-Germany) is *himself the Devil*. The point is crucial because it involves the narrator, whose love and admiration for Leverkühn is the supposed reason for the book's existence, in mutually contradictory attitudes towards his subject. Serenus—who when Adrian is Faust is Faust's Wagner, and when Adrian is Germany is Thomas Mann himself—has a hard fight indeed to sort out in his mind whether his hero is the Devil's victim or the Devil himself: in fact, he does not and cannot do it, because his hero is *both at once*. Very early on in his narrative, Mann tells us he 'yearns' for a German defeat yet does so 'with perpetual torments of conscience'. Serenus interposes to say that the 'special motivation' of this attitude is in his case that in a German victory 'the work of my friend [Leverkühn] would be buried'. Mann then asserts that this is 'only a variant of that which...has become the destiny of a whole people', and that, 'considering the decency of the German character, its confidingness, its need for loyalty and devotion' he 'cannot but cherish a deep and strong resentment against the men who have reduced so good a people to a state of mind which I believe bears far harder on it than it would on any other, estranging it beyond healing from itself'.[67] Now, anyone who has read *Doctor Faustus* will agree without further ado that the character here ascribed to the Germans is pretty well the opposite of that bestowed on Leverkühn, just as it bears very little resemblance to that of the legendary Faustus: the multiple levels of meaning are even thus early in the book contradicting one another. What is the reason for this confusion? It is that Leverkühn's character is framed in accordance with the idea that the Devil is a product of his imagination,

48

i.e. that he is himself the Devil, whereas the above passage is consistent only with the idea that the Devil is real, i.e. that Leverkühn is his victim (the Devil here assuming the shape of 'the men who have reduced' him to incurable self-estrangement).

As the book goes on the text is studded with outbursts against these men:[68] from a human point of view, and from the point of view of Mann's political attitude when speaking in his own proper person, they are entirely justified; but they are not, and cannot be integrated or reconciled with the idea that Leverkühn-Germany is himself the author of his own destruction.

The ambiguity of Mann's feelings towards Cipolla is indeed as nothing compared with the ambiguity of his feelings towards Adrian Leverkühn, the very genius of ambiguity. That he exercises fascination is not merely not concealed, it is emphatically insisted on: Dr Watson is not more completely prostrate before the genius of Sherlock Holmes than Zeitblom is before that of Leverkühn. And yet Adrian is entirely possessed and obsessed by 'daemonic powers', lives a life to which, it is hinted, no kind of filthiness is foreign, is incapable of most normal human relationships, sacrifices his friends to his own ego without the smallest tincture of regret, and ends by being transported to a 'private hospital for nervous diseases' where, to judge from his own account of himself, he should have taken up residence long before: and all this is given the character of 'necessity' so that he may compose a number of works which, if Zeitblom's account of them is to be trusted, are of the most questionable quality and whose human and spiritual content is in any case limited to a reflection and repetition of the sickness of soul that has made their production possible. This double image — transcendent genius and spiritual idiot — never coalesces into a single, three-dimensional one: the narrative brings now this into focus and now that, and the reader is left with the conviction that the author's attitude towards this composite figure is altogether indecisive — in short, ambiguous.

What is the implication of all this for the ideological aspect of *Doctor Faustus*? It is, of course, that as social criticism too the novel is thoroughly ambiguous; that Mann's assertion in his book on its origin that 'Hitler had the great merit of...calling forth a wholly unequivocal No' is in fact untrue: not, of course, in the sense that Mann was lying, but in the sense that what he says in his book on how he wrote *Doctor Faustus* misreports what he says in *Doctor Faustus* itself; and in that event the novel must, on the ground that what the artist says he said is not evidence, be accounted the more trustworthy witness. As a politician, Mann did say No to Hitler, and said it firmly and often; but as an artist whose subject was the nihilism of contemporary Europe in all its aspects his feelings towards the final expression of that nihilism could not be unequivocal. In any event, they *were* not.

3 Decadence

If your idea of what is meant by a fictional character is derived from Shakespeare and Dickens—as, if your native literature is English, it should be—then you will notice when reading Thomas Mann that, although the figures which appear in his novels and stories certainly possess very many characteristics, they are not characters in the Shakespearean or Dickensian sense: that is to say, they are not individuals who, by gradually displaying all the details of their individuality, become types. Mann's characters begin as types and, by having characteristics applied to them, quickly reveal the *concept* in which they originate. It is an altogether different idea of a fictional character. Of those we have already considered, Naphta and Settembrini are most obviously embodied concepts: which is why, whether my elucidation of the concepts they embody be sound or faulty, it is correct in principle. Thomas Mann starts from the idea the character is to represent; the outward form, the thoughts and the words of this character are modes through which this idea can find visible or audible expression; the action in which the character is involved is the conflict between this idea and the ideas embodied in the other characters (or, in the case of the shortest stories, the unfolding of the implications of this single idea). The idea may be simple (Naphta and Settembrini) or complex (Mynheer Peeperkorn). It may be more complex than the author intends (Cipolla) or, presumably because of the emotions associated with it, confused and ambiguous (Adrian Leverkühn). But that all the characters in Mann are in principle reducible to the concept they are intended to embody is the key to an understanding of the kind of fiction he writes—and the reason the kind of analysis which would be heavy-handed and over-literal in the case of *Bleak House* is appropriate and, above all, useful in the case of *Buddenbrooks*, and why it makes good sense to invoke the names of Nietzsche and Schopenhauer in the course of such an analysis—because it was from them that Mann acquired the ideas his characters embody.

If Mann is misunderstood, or not understood, or not understood as well as he might be in the English-speaking world, it is because his English-speaking readers are insufficiently familiar with the ideas whose interplay and conflict constitute the action of his novels and stories. Consider one of his most frequent themes: the conflict between bourgeois and artist, the irreconcilability of the artist and his bourgeois environment. Why this theme? and why is this conflict presented as a conflict between robust health and sanity on the one hand and neurosis and decadence on the other? Why is the bourgeois healthy and the artist decadent?

To answer the first question first: Mann's interest in this theme comes from his immediate experience of it—I mean from the conflict between those elements in his nature which he acquired from his father and those which he acquired from his mother. The double inheritance is very similar to that which Goethe famously declared he had received from *his* parents:

> Vom Vater hab ich die Statur,
> Des Lebens ernstes Führen,
> Vom Mütterlein die Frohnatur
> Und Lust zu fabulieren.

Mann is known to have identified himself very closely with Goethe, especially during his last years, and the above quatrain may partly explain this fact. The details are not exact: Mann's inheritance was not precisely that of his 'stature and the serious conduct of life' from his father and his 'carefree nature and desire to tell stories' from his mother. (Nor was Goethe's own, come to that: there is as much fancy as fact in that famous declaration.) Where the correspondence *is* exact is, of course, in the identification of the father with the serious-minded bourgeois and the mother with the storytelling artist; and in Mann's case this identification accords with reality: his father was an old-style Buddenbrook-type bourgeois and a North German, his mother an artistically-gifted Southerner. But the two sides failed to get on comfortably together: the paternal side had a *bad conscience* about the maternal side—a fact sometimes explicitly stated but in any case palpably evident in the son's writings. As his mother's son Mann was an artist, as his father's a German conservative and bourgeois with a dislike and suspicion of 'artists'.

This was what put him in possession of 'bourgeois versus artist' as a theme for fiction and disposed him to treat this theme in the way he did. The specific *concept* of the artist of which individual artists in his works are more or less exact embodiments came to him from Schopenhauer, modified, as his entire cultural tradition was modified, by Nietzsche.

Schopenhauer's explanation of the nature of the artist is that the production of works of art involves the self-abnegation of the artist's will. 'The intrinsic problem of the metaphysics of the beautiful', Schopenhauer asserts, is: 'how is it possible for us to take pleasure in an object when this object has no kind of connexion with our desires? For we all feel that pleasure in a thing can really arise only from its relation to our will or, as we like to put it, our aims; so that pleasure divorced from a stimulation of the will seems to be a contradiction. Yet it is quite obvious that the beautiful as such excites pleasure in us without having any kind of connexion with our personal aims, that is to say with our will.'

His solution to this problem is that in the beautiful 'we always perceive the intrinsic and primary forms of animate and inanimate nature, that is to say Plato's Ideas thereof, and that this perception stipulates the existence of its essential correlative, the *will-less subject of knowledge,* i.e. a pure intelligence without aims or intentions. Through this, when an aesthetic perception occurs the will completely vanishes from consciousness. But will is the sole source of all our troubles and sufferings. This is the origin of the feeling of pleasure which accompanies the perception of the beautiful. It therefore rests on the abolition of all possibility of suffering.'

The achievement of aesthetic pleasure depends upon a sundering of will from perception, and the achievement of a work of art—i.e. that which produces aesthetic pleasure—depends upon the sundering of will from imagination. If the individual will 'sets its associated power of imagination free for a while, and for once releases it entirely from the service for which it was made and exists, so that it abandons the tending of the will or of the individual person which alone is its natural theme and thus its regular occupation, and yet does not cease to be energetically active or to extend to their fullest extent its powers

53

of perceptivity, then it will forthwith become completely *objective*, i.e. it will become a faithful mirror of objects, or more precisely the medium of the objectivization of the will appearing in this or that object, the inmost nature of which will now come forth through it the more completely the longer perception lasts, until it has been entirely exhausted. It is only thus, with the pure subject, that there arises the pure object, i.e. the complete manifestation of the will appearing in the object perceived, which is precisely the (Platonic) *Idea* of it.'

But this change in subject and object 'requires not only that the faculty of knowledge be released from its original servitude and given over entirely to itself, but also that it should remain active to the full extent of its capacity, notwithstanding that the natural spur to its activity, the instigation of the will, is now lacking. Here is where the difficulty and thus the rarity of the thing lies; because all our thought and endeavour, all our hearing and seeing, stand by nature directly or indirectly in the service of our countless personal aims, big and small, and consequently it is the *will* which spurs on the faculty of knowledge to the fulfilment of its functions, without which instigation it immediately weakens.'

All the everyday affairs of our life are affairs of the will: but in the case of art — 'the perception of the objective, intrinsic being of things which constitutes their (Platonic) Idea and which must lie behind every achievement in art' — the will must play no part at all: 'for only in the condition of *pure knowledge*, where will and its aims have been completely removed from man...can that purely objective perception arise in which the (Platonic) Ideas of things will be comprehended. But such a perception must always precede the conception, i.e. the first, intuitive knowledge which afterwards constitutes the intrinsic material and kernel, as it were the soul of an authentic work of art or poem, or indeed of a genuine philosophy. The unpremeditated, unintentional, indeed in part unconscious and instinctive element which has always been remarked in works of *genius* owes its origin to precisely the fact that primal artistic knowledge is entirely separated from and independent of will, is will-less.'[1]

This, with all *possible* brevity (the length of the above quotations notwithstanding) is Schopenhauer's conception of the origin of works of art and of the aesthetic faculty: it lies in the absence of interest (in the technical sense), in the disengagement and self-annulment of the will. It should be noticed that Schopenhauer derives 'genuine philosophy' from the same source as art, and that what is for him the highest attainment of man, higher even than art and philosophy, namely sainthood, he also derives from the abnegation of the will: the saint is the man in whom all egoism, all personal interest, aim and desire, all *will*, has been annulled. Thus, although his approach and the whole pathos of his philosophy is altogether different from that of Hegel, he comes in the end to agree with Hegel in placing art, religion and philosophy in a special, supreme category of human activity to which every other is inferior.

In Hegel's scheme, these activities constitute the realm of 'absolute spirit', and I shall later (in Chapter VII) examine the influence of this scheme on the structure of *The Magic Mountain*: here we must confine ourselves to the point that, in Nietzsche's philosophy, the artist, philosopher and saint are also very exalted types of humanity (though not the highest type of all), but are so because they embody a very strong and very highly spiritualized form of the *will to power*. In direct riposte to Schopenhauer, Nietzsche asserts that the artist is life-affirmative: 'Artists continually *glorify* — they do nothing else: they glorify all those conditions and things which have the reputation of making men feel good or great or intoxicated or merry or happy or wise';[2] that 'all beauty incites to procreation...precisely this is the *proprium* of its effect, from the most sensual regions up into the most spiritual';[3] and that the *tragic* artist exhibits 'affirmation of life even in its strangest and sternest problems, the will to life rejoicing in its own inexhaustibility through the *sacrifice* of its highest types....Not so as to get rid of pity and terror...but, beyond pity and terror, to *realize in oneself* the eternal joy of becoming — that joy which also encompasses *joy in destruction*.'[4]

It will thus be clear that neither Schopenhauer nor Nietzsche has anything to say against the artist as such, though both distinguish between good and bad artists. But how, then, can Thomas Mann have derived his conception of the artist as *decadent* from them? The answer is that he followed Schopenhauer and not Nietzsche in accounting for the origin of art in an abnegation of the will, but then followed Nietzsche and not

Schopenhauer in viewing abnegation of the will as a mark of decadence. 'Wherever the will to power declines in any form there is every time also...a *décadence*',[5] Nietzsche maintains, and it is in any case true quite generally throughout his philosophy that 'strength of will' is good, 'weakness of will' bad, that 'power' is good, its absence bad. 'What is good?' he asks, and answers: 'All that heightens the feeling of power, the will to power, power itself in man. What is bad? All that proceeds from weakness. What is happiness? The feeling that power *increases* — that a resistance is overcome.'[6] It was a fusion of this idea with the idea that the artist is 'will-less' that produced Mann's conception of the artist as weak, as incapable of a happy existence, as decadent. It must be admitted at once that this fusion is highly illegitimate and 'unphilosophical': Schopenhauer's 'will' and Nietzsche's 'will to power' are conceptions so different in nature that their combination in the manner just described is like mating an eagle and an oak-tree. But we have seen, and shall have occasion to see again, that Mann was no logician and was capable of philosophical blunders of the most thumping description: he was an artist, who used, indeed needed, philosophical concepts in order to set to work, and the mating of an eagle and an oak-tree, impossible in the mundane world, is quite possible in art. As his mother's son, Mann needed to approve of art, as his father's he needed to disapprove of it: Schopenhauer came to the aid of the mother, Nietzsche to the aid of the father. What matter if the union was *philosophically* illegitimate? *Artistically* it was fruitful and that was the main thing. And so the artistic mother's son became an artist and devoted his life to the production of works of art; but the bourgeois father's son got his revenge by making the artist employ his artistry to demonstrate the *decadence* of art.

2

Or — for what is more devious, more full of hidden twists and turns, than the mind of Mann? — or did he *really* get his revenge? Did the mother's son perhaps let him think he had, only to deprive him of it in a way in which he, being merely healthy and philistine, would be incapable of detecting? The first grand instance of artistic sensibility as an expression of decadence is Hanno Buddenbrook, the last of the Buddenbrooks and a mother's son with a vengeance. What an awful, what an appalling child! how incapable of life and how unworthy of it! how sickly, how timid, how *weary*! What does he want, this little Hanno, even before he is out of school? He wants to die: he has had enough of living before he has really begun to live. Life is too much for him, his spirit is too weak to endure it; he needs stimulants even to endure it to the extent he does: better by far if he had not been born. He is everything one means by the word 'decadent', and his artistic giftedness, the one positive quality he possesses, depends upon and derives from his decadence. The artist as decadent: a victory for the father, no doubt about that. Or—*is* it a victory? Did little Hanno appear out of the air? Did he create himself? Was he, even, the son of his mother *alone*? No, of course not, he was a Buddenbrook. He was the son of Thomas, the grandson of Jean, the great-grandson of Johann. Were the Buddenbrooks themselves decadent? Is little Hanno only the unhappy inheritor and *final stage* of a decadence present all along in the Buddenbrook line? Does the artist, by making his artist so extremely exhausted and life-weary a creature—a procedure the bourgeois must, in his blindness, approve of—not also make it certain that this exhaustion must be inheritance, must have been bequeathed to him by his *bourgeois* forefathers?—so that decadence would be precisely that which the artist had in common with them, and his artistic giftedness a form of *strength*, an attempt to surmount his inheritance? Later on the artist will present in one and the same book a serious and a comic confrontation of bourgeois and artist in which each is genuinely the dialectical opposite of the other; but he will not do this until, in *Buddenbrooks*, he has shown how close a relation the artist, the *decadent* artist, is of the healthy bourgeois.

Expressed in terms of the Buddenbrook code, decadence is the inability to subordinate one's natural inclinations and desires to the interests of the family and firm, and that is in the first instance identified with marrying into an inferior class. Bad uncle Gotthold marries a shopgirl, worse brother Christian marries a prostitute; but good son Thomas gives up *his* shopgirl, and good daughter Tony gives up her Morton Schwarzkopf. The short chapter in which Tom says farewell to his girl[7] is our first extended view of him: the contrast with Uncle Gotthold is obvious, as is the fact that, contrary to the clearly expressed opinions of the rest of the Buddenbrooks, the author prefers Gotthold to Thomas. This chapter is, moreover, essentially a preparation for Thomas's self-approving monologue over his uncle's dead body—a speech in which Mann makes his namesake appear utterly odious: 'He came just in time to see the last convulsive motions of the old gentleman. Then he stood a long time in the death-chamber and looked at the short figure under the covers, at the dead face with the mild features and white whiskers. "You haven't had a very good time, Uncle Gotthold," he thought. "You learned too late to make concessions and show consideration. But that is what one has to do. If I had been like you, I should have married a shopgirl years ago. But for the sake of appearance—! I wonder if you really wanted anything different? You were proud, and probably felt that your pride was something idealistic; but your spirit had little power to rise. To cherish the vision of an abstract good; to carry in your heart, like a hidden love, only far sweeter, the dream of preserving an ancient name, an old family, an old business, of carrying it on, and adding to it more and more honour and lustre—ah, that takes imagination, Uncle Gotthold, and imagination you didn't have...And you had no ambition, Uncle Gotthold. The old name is only a burgher name, it is true, and one cherishes it by making the grain business flourish, and oneself beloved and powerful in a little corner of the earth. Did you think: 'I will marry her whom I love, and pay no attention to practical considerations, for they are petty and provincial'? Oh, we are travelled and educated enough to realize that the limits set to our ambition are small and petty enough, looked at from the outside and above. But everything in this world is comparative, Uncle Gotthold. Did you know one can be a great man even in a small place; a Caesar even in a little commercial town on the Baltic?..." Thomas Buddenbrook turned away...He had his hands behind his back and a smile on his intelligent face.'[8]

The insolent repetition of 'Uncle Gotthold' sets the tone: young Thomas thinks he has a right to despise his uncle. But the ground upon which he proceeds to establish this right is, although he does not know it, morally rotten: his instincts have strayed so far from what is naturally desirable and healthy that he can regard giving up the woman you love in order to become a petty-bourgeois Caesar as *good*. One must also add that his conviction that Uncle Gotthold has led an *unhappy* life finds no support anywhere in the novel.

Now just as Tony's aberrant instincts lead her continually to marry the *wrong man*, so Thomas's lead him to marry the *wrong woman*. Gerda Arnoldsen, the daughter of a 'great merchant and almost greater violin artist',[9] is herself a musician, and in fact an altogether typical Mann artist: 'The corridor door opened, and there stood before them in the twilight...a slender figure. The heavy dark-red hair framed her white face, and blue shadows lay about her close-set brown eyes';[10] there is a suggestion of sickliness and nocturnal living about her from the first: 'Thomas Buddenbrook took a solitary breakfast...His wife usually left her room late, as she was subject to headaches and vapours in the morning...[He] met Gerda only at dinner, at four in the afternoon';[11] when she is compelled to rise early her skin looks 'whiter and more even-toned than ever, and the bluish shadows deeper and darker in the corners of her close-set brown eyes',[12] and we are now told explicitly that 'she lived in the twilight of her curtained living-rooms, and dreaded the sun, the dust, the crowds of townsfolk in their holiday clothes, the smell of coffee, beer, and tobacco'.[13] This is 'Gerda, mother of future Buddenbrooks':[14] would that Thomas had married his shopgirl instead—but his instinct for what is good and healthy has decayed too far, he must needs choose and prefer that which he ought most resolutely to have shunned.

Thomas's decadence is pre-enacted very vividly—so vividly as almost to amount to a pre-enactment of Hanno's—in his brother Christian, who inherits the 'bad' tendencies of Uncle Gotthold but, coming a generation later, i.e. a generation further into decadence, has a bad conscience about them and consequently allows them to lead him into neurosis. In accordance with the novel's dialectical scheme he is presented as being artistic. As a boy he reads Cicero while Tom discusses business with their father; as a man he has a passion for the theatre and is a first-rate raconteur: 'he would have held a large audience spell-bound. He narrated like one inspired; he possessed the gift of tongues.'[15] He is clearly an actor *manqué*, and it is natural that he and Gerda should 'get on quite well together'.[16] But as he grows older he becomes more and more subject to nervous disorders and he ends as a mental patient and a grotesque.

59

In him Thomas comes to recognize his own features. During the course of their inevitable final quarrel he tells him: 'I have become what I am because I did not want to become what you are. If I have inwardly shrunk from you, it has been because I needed to guard myself—your being, and your existence, are a danger to me—that is the truth.'[17] This is a very frank admission and in fact nothing less than the moral zenith of Thomas's existence: nothing he has said before or will say again until the very end reveals so great a degree of self-awareness or, rightly considered, of charity towards his brother. But it reveals too that Thomas's strength is the opposite of natural strength: it is more like a terrified reaction or, in terms of the philosophical scheme of another novel, 'fear in the face of pessimism and flight from it', a 'means of self-defence against—the truth'. But the truth will not, in the case of Thomas Buddenbrook at any rate, be for ever put down: at length it gets the upper hand and gives Thomas his quietus. In one of the most famous passages of the novel Thomas, grown prematurely old and tired, gains spiritual enlightenment from a certain book: 'He sat…one day …and read for four hours, with growing absorption, in a book which had, partly by chance, come into his hands…It was a large volume…the second part, only, of a famous philosophical system…He was filled with a great, surpassing satisfaction. It soothed him to see how a master-mind could lay hold on this strong, cruel, mocking thing called life and enforce and condemn it…he struck on a comprehensive chapter and read it from beginning to end…with a concentration which had long been strange to him, completely withdrawn from the life about him. The chapter was called "On Death, and its Relation to our Personal Immortality"…He felt that his whole being had unaccountably expanded, and at the same time there clung about his senses a profound intoxication, a strange, sweet, vague allurement which somehow resembled the feelings of early love and longing.'[18] That night he has an ecstatic revelation founded on the sentiments aroused by this chapter on death and immortality.

What Thomas has accidentally got hold of is the second volume of Schopenhauer's *The World as Will and Idea*, and he was not the only man of his generation to be suddenly enlightened by it. Briefly enough—for the next day Thomas finds it impossible to recapture the mood of the previous night—the philosopher of pessimism has illumined the depths of the official representative of the bourgeois world: the values by which he has tried to live are false; his speech over his dead uncle was vanity and falsehood; his life has been—no, life itself is—a mistake, a long straying in error; and he is exhausted and wants to sink into the voluptuous arms of death. A longing for death which is like the love-longing of youth—the formula of the *Wagnerian pathos*, the Tristan-and-Isolde cult of night- and death-worship—is what from then on alone occupies the soul of Thomas Buddenbrook and is the cause of his sudden and otherwise unaccounted-for expiry. Thomas dies because he desires to die.

The accumulated decadence of the family is at last heaped upon the shoulders of Hanno, who is unable to bear it. He is *altogether* an artist, and is 'artistic-looking' in the most obvious and banal sense; and it is taken for a fact that his artistic giftedness unfits him for the business world into which he has been born. But it is made plain that the traits he bears are merely exaggerations of traits borne by the Buddenbrook line for as long as we have known them. As a concept, an 'idea', Hanno is simply the act of self-abnegation of the will: that which was in the father a sudden and transient vision of salvation from a painful existence is in the son flesh and actuality; that which was for the father a fleeting intuition is for the son a normal state of being. The reader has to deduce for himself that Thomas died because he no longer wished to live, but the novel tells him explicitly that Hanno wants to die: 'Cases of typhus take the following course: When the fever is at its height life calls to the patient...and summons him in no uncertain voice...And there may well up in him something like a feeling of shame for a neglected duty; a sense of renewed energy, courage and hope; he may recognize a bond existing still between him and that stirring, colourful, callous existence which he thought he had left so far behind. Then, however far he may have wandered on his distant path, he will turn back—and live. But if he shudders when he hears life's voice, if the memory of that vanished scene and the sound of that lusty summons make him shake his head, make him put out his hand to ward off as he flies forward in the way of escape that has opened to him—then it is clear that the patient will die.'[19] And Hanno does die: the decadent artist, unfit for life, voluntarily passes out of it. But by that act he also

61

extinguishes the Buddenbrook line—and thereby executes the secret wish and will of a race whose instincts had long before turned awry and led it into courses along which life could be only an error.

3

'The old Kröger family gradually declined, and some people quite rightly considered Tonio Kröger's own existence and way of life as one of the signs of decay.'[20] One should notice the 'quite rightly': *Tonio Kröger* is a sad lyric in which the artist for once tries to describe himself and the pathos of the artist-nature without irony and as a result falls into self-pity. The story is quite rightly one of the most popular in the canon: but there is that about it which characterizes all Thomas Mann's finest stories, the flavour and aroma of 'fine writing'. That Mann was completely master of his medium hardly needs to be said at this time of day, and to read, say, *Death in Venice* for the first time, straight through, is to be lost in admiration for the way in which the writer knows, on the simplest and basic level of his art, how to write. Subsequently, however, one feels even greater admiration for the writer when, conscious of his own mastery, he *puts it at risk* by attempting to extend the boundary of that which it is master over. And he does not merely put it at *risk*, he actually loses it, the former certainty and sureness of step gives place to a heavy-footed gait, an awkwardness and stumbling, as of one who has left the road and walked into the desert; so that the taste which found *Death in Venice* good has to find *The Magic Mountain* in many parts bad. But as the writer has expanded and taken up more into himself, so the taste of the reader has likewise to expand and encompass more, until it can appreciate that deliberate sacrifice of mastery itself as an element in a greater and more worthy whole. This higher and wider taste will then find that which it formerly admired not bad, but *unheroic*, as something domestic, safe, untroubled; it will still admire, but it will now know that the price of 'perfection' is limitation, avoidance of risk, staying at home.

'*In der Beschränkung zeigt sich erst der Meister,*' said Goethe: but did he practice what he preached? *Dämmrung senkte sich von oben* is perfect, *Faust* is very far from perfect, perhaps it is the faultiest 'drama' ever to achieve lasting fame, the ill-made play *par excellence*, but it has that in it which no well-made play could, precisely on account of its well-madeness, ever have, namely the feeling of *heroic life*, of that force which, like nature itself, sacrifices 'perfection' for the sake of profusion, novelty, the wider and wider horizon, the limitless. What do 'mistakes' matter, 'tedium', '*longueurs*', 'bad writing'! It digests them all, as nature digests *its* 'mistakes'. And I venture to say that any writer who has this heroic life in him but does not risk the sacrifice of his mastery in its service must end up in *The Golden Bowl* or with *The Old Man and the Sea*: fine work indeed, none finer; 'perfection', if you will; but safe, at home, miniature: an end, not a new beginning. 'Fine writing' is the *first* achievement of any fine writer: alas if it should be his last achievement also! But with the greatest writers 'perfection' is merely one more ingredient.

Tonio Kröger is 'a very fine piece of writing':[21] a fact that accords very well with its subject, which is a very fine piece of sentimental self-pity: no wonder it has 'preserved its appeal to youth through all the decades since it was written'.[22] Tonio Kröger, a boy with a German surname, an Italian forename, and a dark complexion, is a poet with a bad conscience about being a poet. His verse-making is the subject of criticism by his teachers but also by himself: he 'to a certain extent agreed with those who considered it an unpleasing occupation. But that did not enable him to leave off'.[23] It sounds like a boyish vice, like *the* boyish vice, the same that Hanno Buddenbrook used to practise under the cover of practising the piano. Considering where and when he was born, it is not surprising little Tonio has a bad conscience about it: he is, in fact, deeply worried about his whole psychical condition. At the age of 14 he is in unrequited love with Hans Hansen, a youth with 'straw-coloured hair' and 'steel-blue eyes'[24] and who is bourgeois to the core and cannot, with the best will in the world, take any interest in *Don Carlos* or any other play or poem. Tonio out-grows this youthful passion, and at 16 is in love with Ingeborg Holm, who has a 'thick blond plait' and 'laughing blue eyes'[25] and is, so far as one can judge from the little we are told of her, a goose. Tonio is so confused by her presence that, at dancing lessons attended by the children of the higher bourgeoisie, he makes himself look silly (though not nearly so silly as he imagines), is unable to address so much as a word to her, and wishes he were at home reading Storm's *Immensee* (a very dull piece of work, by the way). Standing outside the room where the dancing lesson is going on he feels himself to be a 'theatre of so much pain and longing'.[26] 'To feel stirring within you the wonderful and melancholy play of strange forces and to be aware that those others you yearn for are blithely inaccessible to all that moves you—what a pain is this!'[27] he exclaims to himself—it is the essence of his predicament. 'But yet he was happy,' the author assures us. 'His heart was full; hotly and sadly it beat for thee, Ingeborg Holm, and his soul embraced thy blonde, simple, pert, commonplace little personality in blissful self-abnegation.'[28] But eventually he falls out of love with Ingeborg as he had with Hans Hansen—or at least he thinks he does; for, since he is as a concept the 'self-abnegation' necessary for the production of works of art, it is not very likely that his feelings will undergo any fundamental change during the course of his life.

He grows up and goes off to live that life: 'and if he went wrong it was because for some people there is no such thing as a right way'.[29] The way the Kröger family goes is the way of the Buddenbrooks: the firm is dissolved, and Tonio is left to shift for himself. He heads south and becomes a writer and nothing but a writer: he lives only to work and feels nothing but contempt for those who work only to live. 'The artist', he declares, 'must be unhuman, extra-human'; he must possess a 'corrupted nervous system'; a 'properly constituted, healthy, decent man never writes, acts, or composes'. Naturally enough, he is 'sick to death of depicting humanity without having any part or lot in it';[30] he longs for 'life, in all its seductive banality', and regrets that the healthy, 'the blue-eyed ones', have no need for or interest in the works of art he produces.[31] The friend to whom he expounds all this silences him by telling him the reason he feels so bad about being an artist is that he is really a bourgeois, 'a bourgeois on the wrong path, a bourgeois *manqué*'.[32] This revelation sets him consciously longing for his old environment and for people with cool, clear names such as Ingeborg—and back he goes to the north. His return to his ancestral home is phantasmagoric: it is no longer real to him nor he to it. He goes further north, to a Danish seaside resort, and there he sees a couple who look like Hans Hansen and Inge Holm: the sight awakens in him the desire 'to be like you! To begin again, to grow up like you...simple and normal and cheerful...to live free from the curse of knowledge and the torment of creation.'[33] He realizes the impossibility of such a new beginning, and in his function as the embodiment of self-abnegation he proclaims that, as Inge had once laughed at him when he made a fool of himself at the dancing lesson, she would be right to go on laughing at him 'even if I...had written the nine symphonies and *The World as Will and Idea* and painted the *Last Judgment*'.[34] After this he confesses, not without placing some strain on one's powers of belief, that 'if anything is capable of making a poet of a literary man [as he deprecatingly calls himself], it is my *bourgeois* love of the human, the living and usual. It is the source of all warmth, goodness and humour.'[35]

Tonio is, of course, Hanno grown up and writing his own story. The decadent family is there but is not insisted on: all the emphasis is on the life-unfitness of the artist himself, and apart from the mildly up-beat ending (a *konzilianter Schnörkel*: see our own last pages) the course of his existence is painful and dreary indeed. What distinguishes *Tonio Kröger* most markedly from *Buddenbrooks*, however, is the uncompromising assertion of the healthiness and attractiveness of the blonde and blue-eyed bourgeois: Hans Hansen and Ingeborg Holm have no function whatever except that of representing North German normality and spiritual soundness; and these are so emphatically and undeviatingly insisted upon that it becomes clear that this function is itself reducible to being merely the dialectical antithesis to Tonio's neurotic decadence: which is to say that, strictly speaking, the story is altogether monothematic, its single theme being the spiritual decadence of the artist as the artist is immediately conscious of it and as this consciousness is heightened when he contrasts it with its opposite. The story's origin in Mann's own circumstances is obvious from the very close similarity between these and Tonio's, and from the direct statement that Tonio's bad conscience about being an artist comes from the bourgeois in him. Mann never made plainer the twofold origin of his conception of the artist as decadent in the facts of his own parentage and the philosophy of Schopenhauer than he did in *Tonio Kröger*.

All this is, together with certain other matters we have not yet touched on, parodied in *Tristan*. This story is a very strange member of Thomas Mann's household: it is a little satyr in whom the family features — the features of those already born and those still to be born — appear in comic distortion. The conflict between artist and bourgeois is so direct and unsubtle as to become crass and grotesque (a parody in advance of *Tonio Kröger*). The theme of the artist's unfitness for life is parodied by making him a visitor to a sanatorium (a parody in advance of *The Magic Mountain*). The Eckhof family as the artist imagines it to be is a parody of the Buddenbrooks. The Wagnerian motif, elsewhere handled with great earnestness, is here reduced to farce in a music-hall version of the love-triangle Tristan-Isolde-King Mark.

The artist, Detlev Spinell, is a ridiculous figure: he is described as a writer, but he has written only one book, 'a novel of medium length', which he keeps open on his tadle 'for anybody to see who entered his room';[36] when Herr Klöterjahn charges in on him for their great showdown he is sitting reading it himself. He has a dark complexion, the soft hairless face of a baby, and 'a halting way of speaking...as though his teeth got in the way of his tongue'.[37] Considering his very modest productivity, his continual assertion of the exclusively artistic nature of his interests looks like a pose, but his conduct makes it clear that, if it was once a pose, it has become reality: one might say that he would be a better man if he were a fraud. The bourgeois Klöterjahn is an equally exaggerated representative of the business world: he possesses 'watery blue eyes shaded by very fair lashes' and speaks in a 'loud, good-humoured voice, like a man whose digestion is in as capital order as his pocketbook'.[38] In contrast to this robust embodiment of crude health and normal appetite, Frau Klöterjahn, born Eckhof, is 'pure and ethereal', but the 'pure, well-nigh transparent spotlessness' of her face is 'dominated quite painfully' by a 'pale blue and sickly' vein which branches out across one of her eyebrows.[39] At her climactic moment playing Isolde's *Liebestod* on the piano her lips became 'colourless and clear' and 'deep shadows lay beneath her eyes', and the 'little pale-blue vein in her transparent brow showed fearfully plain and prominent'.[40]

In these three figures, in Spinell's romanticizings about them, and in the 'romance' between the artist and the artistically-inclined bourgeois wife, the whole world of Mann's fictional interests to that date and beyond it is parodied very comically and without remorse. It is as though the author were ashamed of the sentimental pathos of *Tonio Kröger* and wished to disclaim in advance full responsibility for it. Indeed, when we come to deal with Mann's employment of the style of irony we shall discover that that is precisely the purpose of *Tristan*.

4

The opposition between bourgeois and artist is nowhere more comprehensively asserted than it is in *Doctor Faustus*, where its implications are extended over so wide an area as to make that between Hanno and Tonio and their worlds appear merely *special cases* of this opposition. Serenus Zeitblom is 'the ordinary man'[41] in the broadest sense: he is in every respect 'normal'; Adrian Leverkühn is likewise 'decadent' in the most comprehensive sense: not only is he one of the supreme artists in Mann's fiction, and thus has to embody all the decadent qualities adhering to that condition, he is also outside and set apart in every other possible sense except that of physical deformity. On the novel's literal level, Serenus and Adrian are dialectical opposites. That this opposition does not exclude attraction is something Mann has already made plain in *Tonio Kröger*: the difference here is that it is *the bourgeois who is attracted to the artist*. Tonio's very much more advanced and 'decadent' descendant has no need to tell his own story—Hans Hansen's descendant wants to tell it for him. Another step, a very big step, in the 'decline of a family'.

5

If the artist is in general a decadent, music is the most decadent of the arts. Let us try to see why this is so.

Hanno, the embodiment of the Buddenbrook decadence, is a musician and nascent composer—his mother and his mother's father are also musicians so that he shall be, so that he shall inherit precisely *this* talent. On his eighth birthday he plays to an audience of his relations a fantasy of his own composition, and 'there was an extraordinary contrast between the simple primitive material which the child had at his command, and the impressive, impassioned, almost over-refined method with which that material was employed...He gave every simple harmonic device a special and mysterious significance by means of retardation and accentuation...he sat with lifted eyebrows, swaying back and forth with the whole upper part of his body. Then came the finale...Soft and clear as a bell sounded the E minor chord...It swelled, it broadened, it slowly, slowly rose ...he introduced the discord C sharp...He dwelt on the dissonance until it became fortissimo. But he denied himself...the resolution; he kept it back. What would it be, this resolution...?A joy beyond compare, a gratification of overpowering sweetness! Peace! Bliss!...only not yet—not yet! A moment more of striving, hesitation, suspense, that must become well-nigh intolerable in order to heighten the ultimate moment of joy.—Once more—a last, a final tasting of this striving and yearning, this craving of the entire being, this last forcing of the will to deny oneself the fulfilment and the conclusion, in the knowledge that joy, when it comes, lasts only for the moment. The whole upper part of Hanno's little body straightened, his eyes grew larger, his closed lips trembled, he breathed short, spasmodic breaths through his nose. At last, at last, joy would no longer be denied. It came, it poured over him; he resisted no more. His muscles relaxed, his head sank weakly on his shoulders, his eyes closed, and a pathetic, almost an anguished smile of speechless rapture hovered about his mouth.'[42]

This is almost as explicit as one could be in Germany in 1900, but in case the point has been missed Mann repeats it even more explicitly and with even greater virtuosity of language 280 pages further on. Hanno's schoolfriend Kai asks him if he intends to 'play' that afternoon. The ostensible meaning is 'play the piano', but the question brings a 'flush...and a painful confused look' to Hanno's face. 'Yes, I'll play—I suppose,' he says, 'though I ought not to. I ought to practise my sonatas and études and then stop. But I suppose I'll play; I cannot help it, though it only makes everything worse.' Kai says he knows what Hanno means. 'They were both at the same difficult age. Kai's face burned, and he cast down his eyes. Hanno looked pale and serious.'[43] Obviously they are not talking about playing the piano.

When they get home from school Kai gently urges him 'Don't give up—better not play!' Hanno seems to be immersed in music at home: he plays 'something by Bach' on the harmonium in his room, and after dinner he and his mother play together Beethoven's sonata opus 24. Gerda goes away dissatisfied with the condition of her violin and Hanno is left alone in the salon. It is all depressing beyond words and, as the typical evening of a boy at the 'difficult age' (for so it is presented), gruesomely inappropriate. And then Hanno prepares for some really serious music-making. 'He went to the glass door that led out on the small verandah and looked into the drenched garden. But suddenly he took a step back and jerked the cream-coloured curtains across the door, so that the room lay in a soft yellow twilight. Then he went to the piano. He stood for a while, and his gaze...grew blurred and vague and shadowy. He sat down at the instrument and began to improvise. It was a simple *motif* which he employed — a mere trifle, an unfinished fragment of melody in one bar and a half. He brought it out first, with unsuspected power, in the bass...indicating it as the source and fount of all that was to come, and announcing it, with a commanding entry, by a burst of trumpets...And now there began more lively passages, a restless coming and going of syncopated sound...The syncopation increased, grew more pronounced...This was followed by a tremendous uproar, a wild activity...What was coming?...there was an assembling, a concentrating, firm, consolidated rhythms...Now the music seemed to rouse itself to new and gigantic efforts...an irresistible mounting, a chromatic upward struggle, a wild restless longing ...the flood of rising cacophonies...fought on towards the end that must come, must come this very moment, at the height of this fearful climax — for the pressure of longing had become intolerable. And it came; it could no longer be kept back — those spasms of yearning could not be prolonged. And it came as though curtains were rent apart, doors sprang open...The resolution...burst forth...It was the *motif*, the *first motif*! And now began a festival, a triumph, an unbounded orgy of this very figure...The fanatical worship of this worthless trifle...only a bar and a half in length had about it something stupid and gross, and at the same time something ascetic and religious... There was a quality of the perverse in the insatiability with which it was produced and revelled in...there was a longing for joy, a yielding to desire, in the way the last drop of sweetness was as it were extracted from the melody, till exhaustion, disgust, and satiety supervened. Then, at last; at last, in the weariness after excess, a long soft arpeggio in the minor trickled through, mounted a tone, resolved itself in the major, and died in mournful lingering away. Hanno . . . was very pale, there was no strength in his knees, and his eyes were burning. He went into the next room, stretched himself on the chaise-longue, and remained for a long time motionless'[44] — as well he might.

Even assuming, as one does assume, that Mann could not have described Hanno Buddenbrook masturbating in plain words, one still wants to ask why it is precisely *music* that provides the cover and double-meaning for the description of this act. From the 'soft yellow twilight' in which it is performed, and from the account of its supposed after-effects (which are like the after-effects of an illness or a violent vomiting fit and the account of which could have been accompanied by some mention of the attendant *pleasurable* after-effects) — from this and also on more general grounds, one is bound to assume that, like most people of his generation, Mann regarded masturbation as a perverse, or at best a weakly self-indulgent act, and saw nothing inappropriate in employing regular addiction to it as a major ingredient in the depiction of a decadent personality. It would seem to him, as it did to others, as a sort of passive self-enjoyment of the emotions not merely exhausting and self-exhausting in itself but also tending to inhibit the expression of these emotions outwardly and actively, and thus either a sign or a cause of 'unhealthiness'. Now, 'the self-enjoyment of the emotions' is one way of expressing Schopenhauer's formula for the art of music. In music, he says, the desires and passions, which are the only realities for the will, are the immediate object of aesthetic pleasure: that is to say, the will itself is the object of enjoyment. Music speaks, not of ideas, objects, 'things', but of pure passion divorced from association with any particular object.

Along this line of thought one soon encounters the notion that, whereas sexual desire is normally associated with the object which has aroused it, in music this desire is itself its own object and is enjoyed in and for itself. But since morality can have meaning only in the realm of ideas, music, which exists only in the realm of will, is a *non-moral* art. A poem, a play, a novel must necessarily possess a moral tendency, but music speaks only of that which precedes morality, the desires and passions in themselves. We have already seen Mann take a conception of Schopenhauer's — the 'will-lessness' of the artist —

70

and interpret it in a decadent sense, and now he does the same with Schopenhauer's theory of music. Risking a broad generalization, one might say that, for Mann's generation, sexuality was good if it was 'used' in a morally correct way, bad if it was 'used' in an immoral way, the thing itself being morally neutral; 'self-abuse' was clearly an immoral use of sexuality. (The superstition that it caused physical harm was a consequence of this: in bourgeois morals, the 'immoral' is easily equated with the 'unhealthy' or even with the merely 'not nice'.) Apparently subscribing to this view, Mann then assimilated it to the Schopenhaueran view that music is, as it were, 'self-abuse' in the realm of aesthetics, a 'use' of the aesthetic faculty involving no moral tendency and therefore 'immoral'. To devote oneself to an art which has nothing to do with reason or virtue, which deals only in forces which precede reason and virtue, the primitive forces of the will; to invoke in oneself desires and passions which have reference to nothing but themselves and which can therefore have no objective but their own self-enjoyment: is that not an abuse of the aesthetic faculty, a case of—'self-abuse'? If the decadent Hanno, incapable of meeting life and therefore withdrawing into the closed system of his own subjective feelings, should express himself in art, would the only appropriate art not be *music*, the art in which the feelings enjoy only themselves? And so Hanno has to take up composition and play on the piano free fantasias whose sole content in an onanistic self-enjoyment of their own ardours and raptures—an enjoyment which 'only makes everything worse', i.e. only serves to make the emotional closed system even harder to break out of.

If all this be true, then the champion and advocate of reason and rationality will harbour the greatest mistrust of music: and that, in fact, is what we find him expressing. 'Let music play her loftiest role,' says Settembrini, 'she will thereby but kindle the emotions, whereas what concerns us is to awaken the reason... my aversion from music rests on political grounds.'[45] Music is, like masturbation, a narcotic: that, at least, is the effect it has on Hans Castorp: 'The subdued chords of a hymn floated up; after a pause came a march. Hans Castorp loved music from his heart; it worked upon him in much the same way as did his breakfast porter, with deeply soothing, narcotic effect, tempting him to doze.'[46] Immediately afterwards it is associated with sex: 'He seemed to hear a chase about the room [next door]; a chair fell over; someone was caught and seized; loud kissing ensued — and the music below had changed to a waltz, a popular air whose hackneyed, melodious phrases accompanied the invisible scene.'[47] Later on, while lying in his loggia listening to the sounds of a concert coming up from below and giving 'himself up to the music', Hans 'thought with nothing but hostility of Settembrini':[48] music is now one of the forces taking him away from rationality over to the night side of life. At length, music becomes identified with death: gazing at his own hand behind the X-ray screen and seeing it as it would be when the flesh had rotted from it, 'for the first time in his life he understood that he would die. At the thought there came over his face the expression it usually wore when he listened to music: a little dull, sleepy and pious, his mouth half open, his head inclined towards the shoulder.'[49]

The syndrome of ideas — narcotic, lethargy, sexuality, death — with which music is associated in *The Magic Mountain* and which attains its maximum of intensity in the sub-chapter 'Fullness of Harmony', is the dialectical opposite of rationality, clarity, outgoingness, life: the black art plays the same role here as it did in *Buddenbrooks* and as it afterwards does in *Doctor Faustus*. Serenus tells us that music 'does not seem to me to be included in the pedagogic-humanistic sphere...Rather, it seems to me, in all its supposedly logical and moral austerity, to belong to a world of the spirit for whose absolute reliability in the things of reason and human dignity I would not just care to put my hand in the fire.'[50] To call this an understatement would itself be an understatement: but Serenus is, in his capacity as normal man, given to whimsicalities of this sort, and they are more than made up for in the activities of his friend Adrian, whose career is a demonstration that he who would go to the Devil had better take up composition. Adrian possesses an altogether self-regarding and self-enclosed personality: it follows as a matter of course that he is also a composer, for what art could he practise other than that art whose subject-matter is the enjoyment of itself? On the literal, biographical level Leverkühn is predestined for music: but when Mann seeks to involve the idea that music is the art of decadence with the world of Lutheran superstition to which the Faust legend belongs he overlooks the fact that this idea is *his* idea and not at all the universally accepted idea of the nature of music. The consequence is another case of confusion and mutual misunderstanding between the novel's levels of meaning. When Leverkühn gives up the study of theology in order to study music this is supposed to mean that he has given up God and gone over to the Devil. Now this makes good sense on the literal level provided one does not take the Devil literally (and provided too that the reader already *knows* Mann's attitude towards music—if he does not know it he will fail to see anything at all significant or sinister in this change of faculty). But on the Faust level it makes far less sense, because on this level music cannot be accorded the significance Mann is able to accord it on the literal level.

In this regard it will not be irrelevant to cite Luther's view of music: 'One of the fairest and most glorious gifts of God is music, with which many evil thoughts are banished...Music is the best comfort for a troubled man, it revives and refreshes the heart. Music is a taskmistress which makes people more gentle, more virtuous, and wiser. Youth should always be trained in this art, for it produces cultivated, able people. After theology, I give music the highest place.'[51] Dr Luther would clearly not have seen in Adrian's desertion of theology in favour of music anything of what Dr Mann wants us to see in it: but then Luther had never heard what it seems to me Mann hears whenever he mentions the word music: he had never heard the music of Wagner.

6

The music of Wagner is not only especially potent as a dissolvent of moral considerations, it seems to be what Mann has in mind and ear whenever he thinks of music as the decadent art *per se*, and sometimes even when he thinks of the artist as decadent. We have already noticed the effect of *Lohengrin* on little Herr Friedemann, and we ought to note in passing that Gerda Buddenbrook is 'an impassioned Wagnerite'[52]—another red thread in the pattern of Buddenbrook decadence. (Hanno is also keen on Wagner, of course.) But the first extended treatment of the undermining influence of the Wagnerian art is, very significantly, the parodistic treatment accorded it in *Tristan*.

The story depends for its effect on a knowledge, and in parts a close knowledge, of Wagner's *Tristan and Isolde*; given that knowledge, the effect is incredibly funny. I speak for myself, of course: over what is funny and not funny one can only speak for oneself. The big central scene in which Frau Klöterjahn plays on the piano the best bits of *Tristan and Isolde* — a rendition described partly in the language used to describe Hanno's fantasias and partly by direct quotation from Wagner's text — while darkness and snow fall outside and Spinell works up to an emotional collapse is clearly intended as a *reductio ad absurdum* of the hothouse passion of German romanticism — an *absurdum* which is given a specifically Wagnerian connotation when Frau Klöterjahn's exertions on behalf of Isolde's romantic passion for death lead to her own, very unromantic death.

This parody of bourgeois decadence in terms of Wagnerian romanticism appears again in far sterner form in *The Blood of the Wälsungs*. '*So blühe denn Wälsungen-Blut!*' Siegmund exclaims at the end of the first act of *The Valkyrie*: in his 'study of the mores of Berlin W'[53] Mann shows how this Wälsungen-Blut has 'flourished'. The Aarenhold family is the Hagenströms with the trappings of culture; beneath the trappings they are, like the Hagenströms, barbarians. At the onset of the story they are called to lunch by the 'cannibalistic summons' of the gong, a 'brazen din, savage and primitive'.[54] But this noise is 'out of all proportion to its purport' — which is merely to call the family to lunch — and the house is filled with a 'warm and even atmosphere, heavy with exotic perfume'.[55] They are barbarians, but decadent barbarians. The twin children of the family, rather unsubtly named Siegmund and Sieglinde, are incredibly decadent: Siegmund in particular, called Gigi by his sister, is very far down the road that leads to moral and mental disintegration, a more advanced version of Dorian Gray. They are nineteen and always holding hands. The Hunding of the story, Herr von Beckerath, whom Sieglinde is to marry, is a ninny. The whole family set-up is catastrophically worse than that of the Buddenbrooks at any stage of their history. This, says the story, is what the old bourgeoisie — the bourgeoisie of which Goethe could once be called representative — has become.

On the evening described, Siegmund and Sieglinde attend a performance of *The Valkyrie*, which receives a detailed description on the lines of the description of *Tristan and Isolde* in *Tristan*. Its effect on Siegmund is firstly to make him conscious of the

74

aridity and aimlessness of his existence — 'so full of words, so void of acts, so full of cleverness, so empty of emotion'[56] — but the emotion aroused by *this* music is not one calculated to inspire vigorous outward activity: its tendency is, rather, to heighten the voluptuous self-regard and self-enjoyment which is the most pronounced characteristic of this decaying *Zwillingspaar*. In their carriage on the way home they are as much 'sheltered from the shrill harshness of the bustling life through which they passed' as they had been in their opera-box (or as they are at home, in their lives, in their essential being), and there is still nothing 'which could alienate them from that extravagant and stormily passionate world [of *The Valkyrie*] which worked upon them with its magic power to draw them to itself'.[57] So effective is this power that, when they get home, they imitate their operatic counterparts by committing incest. Is this merely a 'shock' ending, something the reader of 1905 would be startled to find in a story? Not at all: it is the rigorously logical consequence of defining music as the self-enjoyment of the emotions. When they are aroused sexually, Siegmund and Sieglinde instinctively seek satisfaction in one another; the twin-pair, utterly self-engrossed, are the embodiment of a closed system within which the emotions can enjoy only themselves.

4 Irony

Pity is *practical* nihilism.
NIETZSCHE[1]

I

After recording an uncomfortable interview he had with Thomas Mann, Mr Arthur Koestler says that, although his disappointment did not diminish the admiration and gratitude he had always felt for Mann's work, it did seem to offer 'an explanation for a certain aspect of Mann's art which has always puzzled me: I mean the absence of charity.' In Mann's universe 'charity is replaced by irony'. Certain episodes in his life — such as his support for the German war of 1914, the alleged tardiness of his break with the Nazi regime, his acceptance of the Goethe Prize from the East German government — were, according to Mr Koestler, 'symptoms of a bluntness of moral perception, of a defect in ethical sensibility caused by the absence of charitas'.[2]

All readers of Mann are struck by his famous 'ironical style' and the distancing effect — the 'absence of charity' — it produces. Yet I wonder whether the simple conclusion 'absence of charity in the work originates in absence of charity ("bluntness of moral perception") in the author' is not altogether *too* simple. Is it not saying that the cause *must be identical* with the effect it produces? But this 'must be' is not proven, to put it mildly. One is, indeed, inclined to assert the reverse, and say: if the effect is not different from the cause there *is* no 'effect'. In the present case: if Mann had suffered from a 'defect in ethical sensitivity' he would have been incapable of treating ethical subjects ironically — irony being, according to the *Concise Oxford Dictionary*, the 'expression of one's meaning by language of opposite or different tendency'. Perhaps one is even justified in concluding that habitual or obsessive employment of irony would be evidence of extreme, even morbidly exaggerated, sensitivity in respect of that about which one is habitually ironical. Let us, in any event, look more deeply into this question of the 'ironical style' of Thomas Mann.

2

One of his earliest stories is called *Tobias Mindernickel*. Tobias is, like little Herr Friedemann, a grotesque outsider. He suffers from a crippling atrophy of the will: 'he seemed to measure himself against each phenomenon, and find himself wanting; his gaze shifted and fell, it grovelled before men and things'; his whole bearing 'did indeed suggest that nature had denied him the measure of strength, equilibrium and backbone which a man requires if he is to live with his head erect'. He lives alone in 'Gray's Road' and the view from his room is 'hopelessly cut off by the heavy side wall of the next house'; he has no occupation and spends his time sitting and staring at the floor: 'he seemed to have nothing else to do'.[3]

This embodiment of the meaningless is an object of ridicule to the children who also live in Gray's Road. One day a boy who is jeering at him falls over and cuts his forehead; Tobias turns to help him. 'You poor child,' he says as the boy lies bleeding and weeping, '...I pity you', and he binds up his forehead. After this action 'he looked a different man. He held himself erect and stepped out firmly...he looked squarely at people and things, while an expression of joy so strong as to be almost painful tightened the corners of his mouth'.[4] What has happened to Tobias Mindernickel? What has made him happy? Answer: into the meaninglessness he embodies there has been injected—a meaning. What meaning? 'The meaning of life is that it teaches the virtue of pity'—thus spoke Schopenhauer. Tobias has discovered the *supreme virtue*: no wonder he is happy (for virtue makes happy, does it not? We shall see).

He buys a little dog, in order to—what? Love him? Have him for a companion? He thinks so, but his conduct refutes him. He shouts commands at the little dog and when the little dog, unable to understand what is required of him, ignores them, Tobias beats him. After he has beaten him he lets him whimper for a while; but when the dog seems to be imploring forgiveness he picks him up and says: 'Well, I will have pity on you.' Then he breaks down, presses the little animal 'passionately to his breast', stammers out 'You see, you are my only...my only...' and is unable to go on for emotion.[5] What has happened to him now? He has misunderstood the nature of his 'happiness'.

He spends all his time attending to the little dog, but the

feelings he arouses in Tobias are ambiguous: when the dog is happy and high-spirited Tobias is unhappy and beats him; when the dog is dull and melancholy Tobias is pleased and strokes him. One day the little dog accidentally wounds himself on a bread-knife Tobias is holding and falls bleeding to the ground. 'In great alarm Tobias flung bread and knife aside and bent over the injured animal. Then the expression of his face changed, actually a gleam of relief and happiness passed over it.' What has happened? He has *discovered* the nature of his happiness.

He tends the injured dog with great solicitude, but his spirits sink again as the dog recovers. But now he knows why he bought him, and when the dog leaps and jumps about he now follows its movements 'with a sidelong, jealous, wicked look'. He attempts to fondle him but the dog 'was not minded to be pitied'. And because that is so, Tobias seizes him and stabs him again with the bread-knife, this time deliberately. In an instant he is nursing and consoling him, but the dog only 'lay there and rattled in his throat. His clouded, questioning eyes were directed upon his master, with a look of complaining, innocence, and incomprehension—and then he stretched out his legs a little and died.' Whereupon Tobias 'wept bitter tears'.[6] What has finally happened? Tobias has become addicted to pity, so that from being a virtue it has become a vice; but with that the meaning injected into the meaninglessness he embodies is *extracted again*, and when the little dog questions his master there is no answer for him to receive and he dies in a state of 'innocence and incomprehension'. The very thing which, in Schopenhauer's philosophy, is supposed to supply life with a meaning, is here the instrument for making it (if the expression be permissible) even more meaningless.

The story is a very painful one, excessively painful; one wonders how the author could have written it—but one does not wonder that he *never wrote it again*. The little dog's incomprehension—the very epitome of asking Why? and receiving no answer—was *too* painful: thenceforth pain and pity have to be muted, toned down, damped down. With what are they damped down? With *irony*. Irony—the escape-valve of those in whom 'pity' is always threatening to become *excessive*.

What other 'little dogs' are incomprehensibly slain? 'Cases of typhoid fever take the following course'[7]—and then follows, in language from which all emotion has been extracted, an account of a typical death from typhus. In the following chapter we learn, in passing, that it is Hanno Buddenbrook's death that is here being described. 'The pulse raced. Muscular contractions developed and an incipient rigidity of the neck. It was cerebro-spinal meningitis, inflammation of the meninges...a minor symptom was...the squinting of the heaven's blue eyes, caused by the paralysis of the eye muscles accompanying the rigidity of the neck':[8] these technical terms, together with descriptions of the drawing off of spinal fluid and of the patient's shrieks, depict the death of Nepomuk Schneidewein, Leverkühn's little nephew. But no 'poet' would write like that, no poet *could* write like that. 'I am dying, Egypt, dying – of cerebro-spinal meningitis with attendant neck-rigidity and superinduced squint.' Frau von Tümmler, *die Betrogene*, dies of 'hormonal hyperplasia of the uteral mucous membrane, with concomitant haemorrhages'.[9] What is happening here? Why is Mann constrained to render the expiry of these harmless people in such a fashion? As if the clinical physical details of their last illness could serve any purpose or be of any interest whatever – unless they were a cover for something else, for the human details which are even more unpleasing to look upon. Mann examines the spine and the uterus of his dying 'little dogs' so that he shall no more be tempted to look into their *eyes*, and see there the last questioning look of innocence and incomprehension. To describe a death as if one were a pathologist performing a post mortem when one is not a pathologist but a 'poet'; to take from the depiction of death that which the 'poet' is traditionally supposed to provide, namely its emotional and spiritual significance, its 'pathos', its 'grandeur', the shudder and awe those who remain behind experience in presence of 'the departing': why this, unless the 'poet' *can* no longer poetize about death, unless all that is meaningful in death – the pathos, the dreadfulness, the solemnity of death, the feeling that death is a gateway, or a departure, or an awakening, even that it is an 'ending', a conclusion, a summing-up – unless all this has ceased to have meaning because *life* has ceased to have meaning? Mann withdraws sympathetic involvement with his characters – this is the meaning of 'irony' in this instance – because, like Tobias's little dog, he finds their fate incomprehensible.

Imagine what Dickens would have made of the death of

Hanno or of Nepomuk! 'She was dead. No sleep so beautiful and calm...so fair to look upon...Her couch was dressed with here and there some winter berries and green leaves, gathered in a spot she had been used to favour. "When I die, put near me something that has loved the light, and had the sky above it always." Those were her words. She was dead. Dear, gentle, patient, noble Nell was dead. Her little bird...was stirring nimbly in its cage; and the strong heart of its child-mistress was mute and motionless for ever. Where were the traces of her early cares, her sufferings, and fatigues? All gone. Sorrow was dead indeed in her, but peace and perfect happiness were born, imaged in her tranquil beauty and profound repose...The old man held one languid arm in his, and had the small hand tight folded to his breast, for warmth. It was the hand she had stretched out to him with her last smile...Ever and anon he pressed it to his lips...' and so on, pages of it. And Mann? 'Cases of typhoid fever take the following course'; 'Only once in twenty-four hours might the fluid be drawn off, and for only two of these did the relief last. Twenty-two hours of shrieking, writhing torture...Nepomuk Schneidewein...fell on sleep...His parents took the little coffin with them, back to their home.'[10] Of Professor von Rothenbuch, who attends Nepomuk, the author says that he was 'obviously...primarily concerned with the typical progress of the case and a clear clinical picture in all its stages':[11] so, obviously, is the author himself, obsessively. Only, since he is not a physician attending a patient but a novelist writing a novel, his interest is in need of explanation. Dickens could be sentimental about death because for him life had a meaning which gave death a meaning: Mann, however, dare not be sentimental about death, he dare not look into its human face, because life has no meaning and therefore death has no meaning. Dickens is able to suffer with ('pity') his creatures—I am afraid he is, like Tobias Mindernickel, even able to let himself enjoy this sensation—because their suffering has meaning (as a 'test', a 'trial', a 'burden to be borne', a 'penance', a 'punishment', if all else fails as 'the will of God'), and this fact moderates very greatly the pain of the pity he feels. But what could be more painful than pity for *meaningless suffering*? Would it not be *too* painful? Certainly one could not enjoy it—so why should one have it? Where there is nothing to *sanctify* suffering, suffering is mere degrading torment and the sufferer no more than a little dog tortured by a lunatic. Better not to risk the agony pity for *that* would induce: better, far better, to look at it with the eye of irony.

While Nepomuk Schneidewein is going through what could be called the torments of the damned if that word still possessed meaning, Leverkühn declares portentously that the boy's sufferings have convinced him of the futility of human striving: 'What human beings have fought for', he says, '...what the ecstatics exultantly announced—that is not to be. It will be taken back. I will take it back.' When Serenus asks him what he will take back, he replies: 'The Ninth Symphony'.[12] The outcome of this resolve is the anti-Ninth Symphony, Leverkühn's 'last and in a somewhat historical sense his utmost work: the symphonic cantata *The Lamentation of Dr Faustus*',[13] later described as 'the most frightful lament ever set up on this earth'.[14] It is a statement of the meaninglessness of suffering and of life. If Mann had suffered from a 'defect in ethical sensitivity' he would still have been capable of describing it: but would he have made it a lament?

3

The *mechanism of withdrawal* whose literary form is irony becomes a habit: it moves into action of its own accord whenever emotion comes into play. I offer a few examples of this process.

Hans Castorp's father and mother are dead. The death of one's father and mother: that surely is something to inspire emotion. And so: 'His father and mother he had barely known; they had both dropped away in the brief period between his fifth and seventh birthdays; first the mother, quite suddenly, on the eve of a confinement, of an arterial obstruction following neuritis—an embolus, Dr Heidekind had called it—which caused instantaneous cardiac arrest [a 'clear clinical picture']. She had just been laughing, sitting up in bed, and it looked as though she had fallen back with laughter, but really it was because she had died. The father...could not grasp his loss... His spirit was troubled; he shrank within himself; his benumbed brain made him blunder in his business,...while inspecting warehouses...he got inflammation of the lungs. The fever was too much for his shaken heart, and in five days...he died. Attended to his rest by a respectable concourse of citizens, he followed his wife to the Castorp family vault, a charming site in St Katherine's churchyard, with a view of the Botanical Gardens.'[15] The death and burial of one's father and mother after it has passed through the irony-processer.

What did the author's youth mean to him? It meant, one would guess, very much, since Hans Castorp's youth cannot be presented to us until it has been put through the processer whole (the sub-chapter 'At Tienappels' ').

Here is a passage in which the process, usually hidden within the machine, takes place before our eyes. Hans's well-loved cousin Ziemssen has died and, gazing at his lifeless form, Hans is reduced to tears and melancholy reflections: 'he...stood and wept, tears ran down his cheeks...those clear drops flowing in such bitter abundance every hour of our day all over the world, till in sheer poetic justice we have named the earth we live in after them; that alkaline, salty gland-secretion which is pressed from our system by the nervous stress of acute pain, whether physical or mental. It contained, as Hans Castorp knew, a certain amount of mucin and albumen as well.'[16] The 'poetic' is cut away by the introduction of the prosaic ('clinical'): that is the function of the prosaic in the passage, that is why we read of 'gland-secretion' and 'mucin', why in other passages we read of 'typhoid fever' and 'incipient rigidity of the neck' and 'hormonal hyperplasia' and 'Botanical Gardens'. It is so we shall not be compelled to read 'Vale of Tears'.

Every reader of *The Magic Mountain* must have noticed that the language favoured by Hofrat Behrens is a mirror of the author's own ironical manner: one of the best-imagined and realized of Mann's characters, he almost never speaks straightforwardly, almost always distorts his unpleasing communications (what Behrens has to say almost always concerns something unpleasing) in the sense of giving them an ironically humorous twist. Like Mann himself, he seems to want to find the predicaments of his patients rather amusing, and this desire extends to the very least of them: it extends, for example, to 'a Moorish eunuch, a weak and sickly man' — and an utterly minor character — 'who yet, despite his basic and constitutional lack...clung to life more desperately than most, and was quite inconsolable over the conclusions Hofrat Behrens drew from the transparency they made of his dusky inside'.[17] Of course, it is only his outside that is 'dusky': but never mind, he is going to die, so better put him through the processer and have him come out 'quite inconsolable' and the object of a bad joke.

The mechanism continues to work — continues to be needed — until the end. The entire history of Inez Rodde, whose climax is murder and madness, is told ironically (*Doctor Faustus*). The last story of all begins: 'In the twenties of our century a certain Frau Rosalie von Tümmler...was living in Düsseldorf...Her husband, Lieutenant-Colonel von Tümmler, had lost his life at the very beginning of the war, not in battle, but in a perfectly senseless automobile accident, yet still, one could say, "on the field of honour" — a hard blow, borne with patriotic resignation by his wife, who...was deprived not only of a father for her children but, for herself, of a cheerful husband, whose rather frequent strayings from the strict code of conjugal fidelity had been only the symptom of a superabundant vitality.'[18] Or, in other words: 'Frau von T's husband, a military man, died senselessly in a car crash before he was able to die senselessly in battle; but she did not regret his death, because he had long made her life a misery by his habitual adulteries.'

4

Suppose one were to write *Tonio Kröger* without being involved with the hero, without *feeling with* him, how would he appear? The answer is that he would appear like Detlev Spinell, the hero of *Tristan*. Withdrawal of involvement transforms the artist-outsider into a grotesque. Tonio Kröger, cut off from normal society by his inner constitution, becomes a grotesque if sympathy is withheld from him and his predicament. I ask the reader to read Spinell's dotty explanations of why he is staying at the sanatorium and of why he gets up so early in the morning and to consider whether this is not Tonio seen from the funny side; or whether Spinell's letter to Klöterjahn is not Tonio's artistic credo seen from the funny side. 'An odd sort, a very odd sort':[19] but so is Tonio if one cares to look at him in that way, without sympathy.

But before Spinell, before Christian Buddenbrook, little Herr Friedemann is already the artist seen as a grotesque, and not as an amusing one. Like Tonio Kröger he is on the edge of society: he is 'now and then invited out by his schoolmates, but it is not likely that he enjoyed it. He could not take part in their games, and they were always embarrassed in his company';[20] like Tonio Kröger he is forced to renounce normal relations with girls: 'To the others it brings joy and happiness,' he says, 'for me it can only mean sadness and pain. I am done with it;'[21] like Tonio Kröger he consoles himself with art: 'He went home, took up a book, or else played on his violin.'[22] Art becomes for him, as it was to become for Tonio, a substitute for living: 'Music he loved...He came to play the violin not so badly himself...by much reading he came in time to possess a literary taste the like of which did not exist in the place...he knew how to savour the seductive rhythm of a lyric or the ultimate flavour of a subtly told tale.'[23] Under the stress of emotion he comes to recognize this: ' "And how old are you now?" she asked again. "Thirty years old." "Thirty years old," she repeated. "And these thirty years were not happy ones?" Little Herr Friedemann shook his head, his lips quivered. "No," he said, "that was all lies and my imagination." '[24] In other words: 'no, that was not happiness, that was only *art*'.

Where, however, this deformed and frustrated cripple most clearly resembles the romantic Tonio Kröger, so popular with youth, is in his relations with the other chief characters of his story: Johannes Friedemann and Colonel von Rinnlingen are related to one another and to Frau von Rinnlingen as Tonio Kröger and Hans Hansen are related to one another and to Ingeborg Holm, and as Spinell and Herr Klöterjahn are related to one another and to Frau Klöterjahn. In each case the 'artist' keenly desires the woman but is prevented from possessing her by some defect in his nature, while the 'normal man' merely takes her as a matter of course. In the case of Herr Friedemann the woman behaves unpleasantly, but this is because his defectiveness is depicted unpleasantly, i.e. as deformity, and the woman's behaviour merely corresponds. Similarly, the grotesqueness of his fate is merely an artistically appropriate parallel to the grotesqueness of his appearance. All this is surface, plot, accident: in their essentials the lives and misfortunes of Johannes Friedemann and Tonio Kröger are identical. 'Suddenly he was quite overpowered by the strength of his tortured longing. Giddy and drunken he leaned against a lamp-post and his quivering lips uttered the one word' — the word being the lady's name.[25] 'She had come — and though he had tried his best to defend his peace, her coming had roused in him all those forces which from his youth up he had sought to suppress, feeling, as he did, that they spelled torture and destruction. They had seized upon him with frightful, irresistible power and flung him to the earth.'[26] They lead him into courses which result in his humiliation, and he then feels 'a disgust, perhaps of himself, which filled him with a thirst to destroy himself, to tear himself to pieces, to blot himself utterly out'.[27] This tormented creature is little Herr Friedemann, but he could equally well be Tonio Kröger, who also whispered the lady's name into the darkness, was also drawn to her against his will and at the risk of unleashing 'those forces which from his youth he had sought to suppress', never attained his desire and, having reached a state of 'icy desolation, solitude', lay on his bed and 'sobbed with nostalgia and remorse'.[28] In all this they are alike: it is in only one respect that they differ: their creator is *involved* with Tonio, refuses to be involved with little Herr Friedemann — consequently little Herr Friedemann is a grotesque.

The unnamed hero of *The Dilettante* is also the artist-outsider from whom involvement has been withdrawn and who thus appears as a grotesque. His account of himself opens with the word on which the account of Herr Friedemann closed: the word 'disgust'. He too feels nothing but 'disgust...for everything'. Like Hanno and Tonio he is a bourgeois gone rotten: he senses 'the process of dry rot and dissolution going on within', although he grew up in a 'big patrician house, hoary with age'.[29] His mother was 'small and fragile' and played the piano, his father was 'a tall, broad-shouldered gentleman'[30] and did not — with these antecedents he is clearly destined for decadence from birth. Soon it appears: as a child he sits and watches his father and mother, 'and it was as though I would choose between them: whether I would spend my life in deeds of power or in dreamy musing. And always in the end my eyes would rest upon my mother's quiet face.'[31] He takes to playing with a puppet theatre — 'up to my thirteenth or fourteenth year this was my favourite occupation'[32] — and graduates to verse-writing and music. He is doomed. In the course of a few paragraphs the family business goes broke and the mother and father die comic-pathetic deaths (notice that all this *precedes Buddenbrooks* and is consequently another instance of anticipatory parody). He recognizes himself to be 'a perfectly useless human being',[33] and after a brief period of travel he settles down to 'a life of quiet and contemplation'.[34] One day he sees and falls in love with a young lady who, it turns out, is on the point of becoming engaged to a young man whose outstanding characteristic is naive self-confidence and self-possession. It is the triangle with which we are now familiar. The dilettante is incapable of making the slightest advance to her: and when he sees her in a box at the opera in the company of the self-possessed young man he feels 'shut out, unregarded, disqualified...pariah, a pitiable object even to myself'.[35] At length he visits a charity bazaar at which the young lady is assisting — she is selling wine and lemonade — with the objective of striking up an acquaintanceship with her, but when he does summon up the courage to approach, 'hatred and helpless hapless misery prevented me from looking at her at all, and in desperation I carried through my stout resolve by saying gruffly, with a scowl and in a hoarse voice: "I'd like a glass of wine" '.[36] After this final revelation of his contemptibleness, he resolves on suicide but realizes he will never have the will to carry out his resolve.

There is no need to flog the point that this is in all essentials Tonio Kröger become grotesque through withdrawal of involvement: the fact is obvious. Less obvious, probably, is that the monk Hieronymus in *Gladius Dei* is also the artist-outsider in grotesque shape.

The Savonarola face, the dark habit, the unheeding gait mark him as a man apart, the 'radiant' and art-loving city of Munich renders him by contrast grotesque. He is altogether out of place, a figure from another age. His 'story' is simply his unsuccessful attempt to persuade an art dealer to remove from his window a popular painting of the Virgin which offends his susceptibilities. At first it seems that these susceptibilities are entirely religious, but as the somewhat one-sided conversation proceeds it appears they are artistic as well. 'Art is no conscienceless delusion, lending itself to reinforce the allurements of the fleshly', he declaims, reinforcing his objection to the painting. 'Art is the holy torch which turns its light upon all the frightful depths, all the shameful and woeful abysses of life; art is the godly fire laid to the world that, being redeemed by pity, it may flame up and dissolve altogether with its shames and torments.'[37] The face is Savonarola's face, but the voice is the voice of Schopenhauer—or again of Tonio Kröger as he voices his contempt for the part-time artist, the trifler and dilettante who does not know that 'one must die to life to be utterly a creator'.[38] 'He could not endure the blithe and innocent with their darkened understanding, while they in turn were troubled by the sign on his brow.'[39] This is Tonio, but it could just as well be Hieronymus, the black-hooded monk darkening with the shadow of his presence the radiant city of Munich.

5

Granted most of us never seriously doubt that other people are real, are actually there before us: what is it in us that seems to guarantee their reality? Answer: the feelings we have about them. If our feelings about them are intense (if we feel love, hate, envy, pity), they will be intensely real to us; if our feelings are only mild or if we feel hardly anything at all, they will be much less real. To a man who has no feelings about other people, whose feelings are all self-directed—the purest modern example is Hitler—other people will possess no reality: he will see them and hear them and shake hands with them, but he will never *meet* them—his 'meetings' will be between himself and the not-himself, i.e. the outside world, in which men and the material universe are indistinguishable, being merely the boundary of the self. This is true in life; it is also true in art. If an author creates characters and then withdraws from them the feelings he has about them they will become less real. Spinell is less real than Tonio Kröger: the latter is a possible human being, the former a caricature. The transformation of the artist into a grotesque is a movement away from reality—this effect being, of course, the intended purpose of this transformation. But the grotesque human being in a real world—the situation depicted in *Little Herr Friedemann, The Dilettante, Tristan, Gladius Dei*—is only a first step: *the world too must become grotesque.* And here we touch on the most far-reaching effect of the 'ironical style': the transformation of reality into phantasmagoria.

Thomas Mann's characters are inordinately given to *dreaming.*

Hans Castorp starts to dream the moment he falls asleep on his first night on the magic mountain. He dreams about the people he has just met: they reappear in grotesque shape — and since we too have only just met them their reintroduction in this shape at once begins to reduce their substantiality. On his second night he experiences 'even more involved' dreams than on his first; indeed, he dreams constantly, and sometimes his dream feelings are more real to him than his waking — they are even 'a thousandfold stronger'.[40] Thirty years later, Felix Krull, on a train to Lisbon, has a 'series of confused dreams'[41] in which the subjects of Professor Kuckuck's illuminating conversation take on visible form. But these avowed dreams, and the many others like them, are none the less exceptional in that they *are* avowed. It is the unavowed dream, the waking dream, that arouses our suspicions as to the artistic purpose of all this dreaming.

Consider, as an exemplary instance, *The Wardrobe*. Albrecht van der Qualen alights from a train, he knows not where. He has been asleep, but he knows not for how long. He does not know what time of day it is. He is a sick man and likely to die at any moment. As he walks through the unknown town he feels utterly detached: 'I...am as alone and as strange as probably no man has ever been before', he tells himself. 'I have no business and no goal...I owe nothing to anybody, nobody owes anything to me. God has never held out His hand over me, He knows me not at all.'[42] For no reason he rents a room in a lodging house. The landlady has 'a sunken birdlike face and on her brow there was an eruption, a sort of fungus growth. It was rather repulsive.' Van der Qualen tells her: 'You are like some kind of banshee, a figure out of Hoffmann, madame.'[43] The wardrobe in the room has no back and stands in an unused doorway, so that it would be possible to enter it from behind. When Van der Qualen, preparing for bed, opens this wardrobe he finds a beautiful naked woman in it: he invites her out, but she refuses to come out and offers to tell him a story. The way the story is told suggests Albrecht is telling it to himself 'in the half-slumber of fever':[44] it describes, briefly enough, how one of a pair of lovers kills the other. From now on the woman appears every evening and tells him stories; and sometimes she does come out of the wardrobe. How long this goes on the author will not tell us. He suggests it may all be a dream. He implies that Albrecht van der Qualen may be dead. In any event, the whole action is phantasmagoric: and its ambiguities are not meant to be resolved. But even if the submerged 'real story' were elucidated — and I do not doubt this has been done — it would still not interest us very much: what is interesting about *The Wardrobe* is that it is a tolerably successful exercise in transforming the real world into something unreal, a *waking* dream.

The life of Thomas Buddenbrook is reality becoming waking dream: the matter-of-fact world into which he is born is made, by a wide range of devices and over a long period, to dissolve into the indefinite, hard-to-grasp, phantasmagoric. The normal becomes uncanny, the real slides away, one no longer knows where to place one's feet or one's feelings. In the end one withdraws one's feelings, because they no longer have anything to attach to. And all this is, of course, entirely in accordance with the author's wishes: because Thomas's death must be, like every death, meaningless, he wants us to lose all real feeling for him before he is obliged to have him die.

We are given a preview of this meaningless death in a life become unreal in the grotesque death of Senator Möllendorpf: 'James Möllendorpf, the oldest of the merchant senators, died in a grotesque and horrible way. The instinct of self-preservation became very weak in this diabetic old man; and in the last years of his life he fell victim to a passion for cakes and pastries. Dr Grabow, as the Möllendorpf family physician, had protested energetically, and the distressed relatives employed gentle constraint to keep the head of the family from committing suicide with sweet bake-stuffs. But the old senator, mental wreck as he was, rented a room somewhere, in some convenient street, like Little Groping Alley, or Angelswick, or Behind-the-Wall — a little hole of a room, whither he would secretly betake himself to consume sweets. And there they found his lifeless body, the mouth still full of half-masticated cake, the crumbs upon his coat and upon the wretched table. A mortal stroke had supervened, and put a stop to slow dissolution.'[45]

This death is grotesque but it has a cause: Thomas's death is also grotesque but it has no apparent cause. 'Senator Buddenbrook had died of a bad tooth. So it was said in the town. But goodness, people don't die of a bad tooth! He had had a toothache; Herr Brecht had broken off the crown; and thereupon the Senator had simply fallen in the street. Was ever heard the like?'[46] This is what was said in the town, where people know only the outer shell of Thomas Buddenbrook; but we, who have been admitted into his soul, know that the 'bad tooth' was merely the essential 'clinical detail': what was really bad was precisely the soul. Life had become unreal, uncanny, unfamiliar, and he wanted to be out of it. What Thomas suffers from is not merely toothache—although he suffers from that, too, and so does the reader, and without anaesthetic: no, toothache is a symptom of 'soul-ache', the weariness of the overtaxed soul. Everything has gone wrong, rotten, bad; life itself, he has just to his great relief discovered from Schopenhauer, is *essentially* bad, a bad dream, a fever-dream, an excrescence on the calm face of nothingness, it is itself nothing, a phantom, unreal. How easy to abolish the unreal: even a toothache can be fatal to it! And so Thomas—in whom the 'instinct of self-preservation' has not merely become very weak but has actually turned against itself, has become the desire for self-destruction—can die of next-to-nothing because for him life has become next-to-nothing.

What in the end is left of the former Thomas Buddenbrook? One thing only: his lifelong scrupulosity in dressing. And it is this which is reserved for the last transformation—a transformation which reveals that it had all along existed only so that it might at last be thus transformed. When he falls dying, he falls in a dirty street, and is brought home covered with filth. 'Gerda Buddenbrook's lovely white face was quite distorted with horror and disgust; and her close-set, blue-shadowed brown eyes opened and shut with a look of anger, distraction, and shrinking..."How he looked...when they brought him! His whole life long, he never let anyone see even a speck of dust on him—oh, it is insulting, it is vile, for the end to have come like that!" '[47] Yes, it is plainly apparent that Thomas Mann does not wish to feel very deeply moved by the death of Thomas Buddenbrook.

The total transformation of reality into phantasmagoria—essayed on a small scale in *The Wardrobe*—is achieved much more successfully and on a much larger scale in *Death in Venice*. The narrative style of this story is, as is usual with Mann, characterized by a close attention to details—but these details, when closely observed, now serve to deprive the narrative of all realism and to transform it into fantasy, as though the real world were being seen through the sick eyes of Gustav von Aschenbach.

At the beginning of the story Aschenbach, the famous and respected author, feeling unwell takes a walk through the streets of Munich. He halts before a mortuary chapel decorated with such scriptural texts as 'They are entering into the House of the Lord' and 'May the Light Everlasting shine upon them'; here there suddenly appears before him 'a man standing in the portico, above the two apocalyptic beasts that guarded the staircase'. He cannot decide how the man has got there, but he observes him minutely, and the narrator gives us a close description of the man's dress and features.[48] As a consequence of this experience Aschenbach feels 'a longing to travel' so strong as to resemble 'a seizure, almost a hallucination'.[49] The man's dress bears some resemblance to hiking gear, but the connexion between his appearance and Aschenbach's reaction is not naturalistic: the apparition has, for whatever reason, sent him on the route to his death.

Where he is to die is stated immediately: reflecting on the number of places he can travel to, he has a vision of 'a tropical marshland, beneath a reeking sky, steaming, monstrous, rank — a kind of primeval wilderness-world of islands, morasses, and alluvial channels...Among the knotted joints of a bamboo thicket the eyes of a crouching tiger gleamed — and he felt his heart throb with terror, yet with a longing inexplicable.'[50] The fragmentary repetition of this description at later points in the story reveals that what he has visualized is Venice become a 'morass' through the invasion of the 'Asiatic' cholera, and the source of the disease itself, 'the hot, moist swamps of the delta of the Ganges, where it bred in the mephitic air of that primeval island-jungle, among whose bamboo thickets the tiger crouches'.[51] Aschenbach's inexplicable longing is for death.

The figure between the apocalyptic beasts which sends him out to meet death reappears twice: the first time as the un-licensed gondolier who ferries him from his boat across to the death-trap of Venice, the second time as the singer who performs in front of the hotel, smells of carbolic and passes on the cholera.

In all of this there is nothing whatever naturalistic. Aschenbach moves as if in a dream: the dreamlike atmosphere is reinforced by a hundred details. On the boat to Venice he meets a prefiguration, altogether unreal but entirely in place in a scene of phantasmagoria, of his own final condition before death claims him: 'Aschenbach...was shocked to see that the apparent youth was no youth at all. He was an old man...with wrinkles and crow's-feet round his eyes and mouth; the dull carmine of the cheeks was rouge, the brown hair a wig.'[52] Even as he is experiencing the events of the voyage, Aschenbach feels 'not quite canny, as though the world were suffering a dreamlike distortion of perspective'.[53] The gondola is 'black as nothing else on earth except a coffin' and as he steps into it, it calls up in him 'visions of death itself, the bier and solemn rites and last soundless voyage';[54] he finds it so comfortable he wishes the trip 'might last forever'.[55]

Arrived in his graveyard, Aschenbach begins a long and one-sided romance with the life is he about to depart from. The boy Tadzio is described in dozens of phrases which are all merely variants of one phrase: that he is 'beauty's very essence'.[56] That he is 'real' no one will suppose: that on his first appearance Aschenbach remarks on the contrast his 'perfect beauty' presents to the plainness of his sisters suggests that Aschenbach is bestowing something if not all of this beauty on him himself. His attempted flight from Venice is thwarted by an accident which, as in a dream, is the fulfilment of his own desire; his trip back there is, unlike the first trip, swift and easy: no resistance of any kind is left.

The second stage of Aschenbach's death is written up in language that now frankly abandons the descriptive manner and becomes inordinately florid, baroque and 'mythological': 'Now daily the naked god with cheeks aflame drove his four fire-breathing steeds through heaven's spaces',[57] and so on. Aschenbach as an individual begins to disappear within the mound of words heaped up around him: the concept he embodies is developed more luxuriantly than a 'character' can well survive. The nearer he approaches the end the less restrained is his worship of the beauty he has created and the more unbalanced and 'decadent' does he himself become. At length the baroque manner, overborne by the fantasy it is seeking at once to communicate and suppress, gives way to undisguised phantasmagoria, and Aschenbach, after a terrific erotic dream in which the contents of his decaying soul are vomited up, abandons all restraint and all 'normality'. His love of 'Tadzio' has already forced him to notice how old he is getting: now, as prefigured by the young-old man on the boat, he resorts to cosmetics and becomes a parody of his own ideal of youth and beauty, while the boy, as if to emphasize the grotesqueness of his elderly admirer, grows ever more ethereal. Trailing Tadzio through the narrow streets of Venice, 'where horrid death [cholera] stalked too', it seems to him 'as though the moral law were fallen in ruins and only the monstrous and perverse held out a hope'.[58] He lives as in a dream, and when he talks to himself 'the rouged and flabby mouth uttered single words of the sentences shaped in his disordered brain by the fantastic logic that governs our dreams'.[59] The last thing he sees before his decease is pure dream: Tadzio, standing on the seashore, beckons him out into the ocean of nothingness. And with that he is dead.

On the level of realism, the plot of *Death in Venice* is: an elderly and much admired and respected author is tired from overwork; he decides to take a holiday and goes to Venice; there he sees a beautiful boy who arouses in him repressed homosexual feelings of which he is ashamed; he indulges in fantasies about the boy, at first sublimated and artistic (Greek statues and the like), later frankly erotic; but because he has a bad conscience about all this his morale is destroyed and his outward behaviour begins to correspond with his inner constitution. At the same time Venice is invaded by cholera, and the progress of the physical disease parallels that of his psychological and spiritual degradation. This plot—which, although somewhat lurid, is of course in no way impossible in the real world— is made to bear a weight of *leitmotif*, fantasy and 'fine writing' which pushes it down out of the real world into the underworld of dream and phantasmagoria: and this procedure is an extension and consequence of what is in the long run the most striking thing about the story—the total lack of sympathy evidenced for the wretched Aschenbach. As Tonio Kröger is Hanno grown up, so Aschenbach is Tonio grown old. But his author now refuses to enter into him sympathetically: he is viewed with the eye of irony and he is as a consequence transformed into a grotesque and the world in which he moves loses its reality.

6

Distance—this is the objective: to place between the feelings of author and reader and the objects to which these feelings might attach themselves a curtain of mist—of allegorizing, fanticizing, argufying, leading-motivizing—so that these objects may *recede*, grow less substantial, become unreal. Aschenbach's death in Venice—as meaningless a death as any man could well die—must not be allowed to affect us emotionally; we must not be able to 'pity' him; consequently he and his world have to become distant and unreal.

The story is a substantial effort, but it is still a performance on a restricted scale when compared with that which followed in *The Magic Mountain*: and if the little Venetian bathing-beach is hidden behind a haze of heat, the way up to the sanatorium Berghof is shrouded in fog. Let us look at some of the ways in which the 'real world' is obscured, made distant and fantastic, in *The Magic Mountain*.

We are presented very close to the beginning with an image which the reader of the novel ought to keep somewhere in his mind until the end. Hans Castorp, standing beside the bier of his dead grandfather, becomes 'distinctly aware, though without admitting it in so many words', that all the decorative objects set around the bier, 'but expressly the flowers, and of these more expressly the hosts of tuberoses, were there to palliate the other aspect of death, the side that was neither beautiful nor exactly sad, but somehow almost improper—its lowly, physical side—to slur it over and prevent one from being conscious of it'.[60] The odour of tuberoses obscures the odour of the corpse—a deception paralleled by the healthy glow on the faces of the tuberculosis patients at Haus Berghof, and by the whole technique employed to tell the story of the events on the magic mountain.

On his first full day at the sanatorium Hans begins to feel ill. What is the chief symptom of his illness? It makes his surroundings seem distant and unreal.[61] The effect persists and grows stronger: soon he is momentarily unable to remember how old he is, and seeking to describe how he feels, he says: 'Do you know how it is when you are dreaming, and know that you are dreaming, and try to awake and can't? That is precisely the way I feel.'[62] The scenes he visits often appear to him 'dreamlike';[63] finally he says he regards what he and Madame Chauchat 'had together' as 'a dream'.[64]

This long-drawn-out romance is indeed dreamlike and fantastic: it resembles a fantasy Hans Castorp is enjoying in the privacy of his own imagination. Its onset is an extended vision of an incident in Hans's youth which the author does everything he can to make seem magical: his schoolboy 'affair' with Pribislav (pronounced Pschibislav) Hippe. The recollection of this past affair is far more lively to Hans than the present reality around him, and it subsequently colours all his feelings towards Clavdia Chauchat—in fact, it is really with Pribislav Hippe that he has his subsequent romance at the Berghof; it is only in so far as she resembles Hippe that Clavdia exercises any attraction upon him (indeed, the author informs us, 'resembled was not the word: they were the same eyes...everything was precisely Pribislav, and no differently would he have looked at Hans Castorp were they to meet again as of old in the school court-yard'.[65]) Hans suffers torments for 'love'—torments which are never described except in a tone of indulgent and mildly amused irony—but his love is for a phantom, and that his 'affair' should be consummated on 'Walpurgis Night' is simply the consequence of its phantasmagoric nature.

The complete reduction of the Berghof and its occupants to unreal phantoms which is the essential purpose of 'Walpurgis Night' is pre-figured by a visit to the cinema: 'It was a thrilling drama of love and death they saw silently reeled off...full of cruelty, appetite, and deathly lust...constructed, in short, to cater to the innermost desires of an onlooking international civilization...But when the last flicker of the last picture in a reel had faded away, when the lights in the auditorium went up, and the field of vision stood revealed as an empty sheet of canvas, there was not even applause. Nobody was there to be applauded.'[66] Shadows whose loves and deaths, however thrilling, are only the loves and deaths of shadows: is it these, perhaps, which also inhabit the magic mountain?

A few pages later Walpurgis Night arrives. Mann hammers home relentlessly the equation of the Shrove Tuesday celebrations at Haus Berghof with the Walpurgis Night scene in *Faust*. For the first time the words 'magic' and 'mountain' are brought into association via a quotation from *Faust*:

Allein bedenkt : der Berg ist heute zaubertoll.[67]

'The mountain is magic-mad today' — and indeed there is only one 'magic mountain' known to German legend and that is the Brocken: and that, clearly, is where we are. Settembrini, who quotes from the *Faust* Walpurgis Night scene all but incessantly, equates Hofrat Behrens in carnival garb with 'Herr Urian', the leader of the witches' rout, and Behrens' superiority over the other phantoms is visibly demonstrated in his superior ability to draw a pig. The identification of the carnival with a witches' sabbath is altogether unquestionable: and its purpose is to reduce our sympathetic involvement with the fate of the participants and to shake our belief in the reality of the world they inhabit.

Now, another of the literary sources of *The Magic Mountain* contains an even closer verbal association of 'magic' and 'mountain' than the line from *Faust* quoted above: in *The Birth of Tragedy* the actual word *Zauberberg* — magic mountain — is used to describe Mount Olympus.[68] We have already seen how the phantasmagoric dream in the sub-chapter 'Snow' derives from *The Birth of Tragedy* and its concept of civilization as the sublimation of ferocious and bestial drives, and how, as a result of reflecting on this dream, Hans resolves that, 'for the sake of goodness and love', he will henceforth 'let death have no sovereignty over his thoughts'.[69] But it was to attain precisely this end, Nietzsche says in *The Birth of Tragedy*, that the Greeks created the Olympian pantheon: 'The same drive that materialized in Apollo generated the whole Olympian world' — and with that insight, he says, 'it is as if the Olympian *Zauberberg* had opened before us and revealed its roots to us'. What was the 'tremendous need' which generated Olympus? 'The Greek knew and felt the terrors and horrors of existence: in order to be able to live at all he had to set before it the glittering dream image of the Olympians...Wherever we encounter the "naive" in art, we have to recognize the most potent effect of Apollonian culture, which always has first to overturn an empire of Titans, and kill monsters, and, by means of powerful and joyful illusions, triumph over a dreadful insight into the depths of reality and in intense susceptibility to suffering.'[70] Does this not tell us something about Thomas Mann's *Zauberberg* and the 'powerful and joyful illusions' which inhabit it? and about why they *are* illusions and phantoms, and not reality? The words that herald the end of the novel—the reference to the 'thunder-peal' that was 'the shock that fired the mine beneath the magic mountain, and set our sleeper ungently outside the gates', so that he 'sits in the long grass and rubs his eyes'[71]—do these words not suggest, behind the obvious metaphor, that our entire sojourn on the mountain has been a dream and illusion? an Apollonian dream and illusion born of and necessitated by 'an intense susceptibility to suffering'?

7

The magic mountain is Olympus and the Brocken: the illusory and phantom world, light and dark, which the artist substitutes for the real world. But, although an illusion it is—one may risk this adjective—a playful illusion: the glitter of sun on snow and the cold thin air proper to the heights is never very far away. Anyone who has lived in these regions will know from experience that a hangover cannot last very long in that morning air, that the 'spirits' of the night are easily exorcised. Golo Mann called *The Magic Mountain* 'a delicately carved puppet-theatre',[72] and that description, since it suggests the playful and well-lit, is not far from wrong. Now, turning away from that cultivated and urbane entertainment, prepare to enter the cabinet of Dr Caligari.

Here there is no light or air: it is stuffy, horribly stuffy, and when the blackness is occasionally broken it is by a flickering green illumination which reveals that we are surrounded, not by 'phantoms' or even by puppets, but by motionless cardboard figures whose painted grimaces are not so much frightening as conventionally horrific. The more I reflect on *Doctor Faustus* the more I become convinced it is the last and by far the most valuable product of the German expressionist cinema. It would, indeed, make a superb film, but only on condition that fidelity to its details was absolute. No romanticizing of

Leverkühn! He is the very Devil: conscienceless self-assertion ('creativity'). To speak of phantasmagoria in this case would be to suggest too great a degree of substantiality: the figures one sees are cards jerked up into the artificial light and then jerked away again, or, precisely, images projected on to a cinema screen. A 'phantom' has behind it the mind from which it proceeds: but what do these cards, these projected images, have behind them? A blank screen, nothing. And considering that the true theme of the novel is the consummation of European nihilism this effect is not merely appropriate but the only effect that could actually transmit this theme and not merely describe it. *Doctor Faustus* is thus that very rare artefact, a novel which *is* what it is about—and that is why the things that are 'wrong' with it may, as I suggested earlier, be wrong only in so far as they produce ambiguity.

The difficulty is to decide how much of *Doctor Faustus* is the result of the author's conscious intention. Taking into account all one knows of Mann, my own feeling is that his intention was, before all, to express the sense of *total catastrophe* which filled him when he contemplated the recent history of his country, and that this intention persisted within the complicated structure he erected and ended by *undermining* it, so that the catastrophe he was describing actually overtook the novel in which he was describing it: all the novel's 'faults'—the cardboard characterization, the obsessive borrowing and the debasement of what is borrowed, the overwriting (an exaggeration of a standing trait), the deluge of factual information (ditto), the life- and airlessness, the contradiction between differing 'levels of meaning'—are at once the product and the completest expression of its theme.

Nihilism has, like infinity, its own laws, under which what is otherwise illogical becomes, not logical, but simply the case: it is the case, for example, that in infinity the number of even numbers is the same as the number of all whole numbers, although 'logically' there should be only half as many; and it is also the case that a 'faultless' novel about a nihilistic collapse would utterly fail to communicate its theme, although 'logically' a faultless novel would be one which communicated its theme most completely. Leverkühn, to take the central character and central failure, is not merely not a complete human being, a believable figure, he is not even put together 'logically' in the manner of Frankenstein's monster: he has, so to speak, two heads and too many limbs, he is not believable even as a monster. There is no question of feeling sympathy for him, not even the inverted sympathy of revulsion: he does not exist sufficiently to arouse any feelings. The reader is constantly distracted from the 'character' by being compelled to notice the sources from which it is being drawn. In the end he is, as already remarked, simply conscienceless self-assertion: all his other characteristics belong to someone else, this alone stays with him and is his. By any standard—the standard set by Mann's own characters very much included—Leverkühn is a failure: but since he is the central figure of a novel whose subject is the nihilistic collapse of civilization and European culture and morality he is the only protagonist who would be adequate, and is consequently also a success, one may even say an incomparable success. And the same is true of every other 'failure' of the novel.

It is unquestionable that the evocation of an air of unreality, of oddness, of a Caligari's cabinet of grotesques, is part of the author's *conscious* intention. Consider only the names bestowed on the characters: Serenus Zeitblom, Wendell Kretschmar, Ehrenfried Kumpf, Eberhard Schleppfuss, Rüdiger Schildkapp, Monsignor Hinterpförtner, Nepomuk Schneidewein, Rudolf Schwerdtfeger, Dr Helmut Institoris, Sextus Kridwiss. Some of them are meaningful, but all of them are, before all, odd. In one place the author refers to the 'frightful bombardment of the city of Dürer and Willibald Pirkheimer':[73] if the reader does not know who Willibald Pirkheimer is it does not matter— the effect, surely intentional, of juxtaposing one of the most famous and euphonious of names with one obscure and quaint-sounding is to reinforce the atmosphere of grotesqueness to which all the other names contribute. Many of the characters are said, like many in *The Magic Mountain*, to be modelled on real people: some one can recognize, some one cannot. Presumably if one were able to recognize them all one would have a larger grasp of the level of the novel on which Adrian represents Germany; but the canvas is already very crowded, and the knowledge that, for example, Schleppfuss ('drag-foot') is supposed to be, in addition to himself, the Devil and the club-footed Dr Goebbels, is sufficient to persuade us that to dig out the double and triple identity of each of the characters would be merely to add needlessly to existing confusions and ambiguities. The central phantasmagoria, that peculiar to Leverkühn, is doubly unreal: I mean that, even on the level of very much modified reality upon which the narrative exists, it is regarded as being exceptionally bizarre. His interview with the Devil is a piece of 'unreality' even on the linguistic level, the language in which it is written being a parody of 'Lutheran' German studded with quotations from Nietzsche. But this is by no means all: for when, in his final address to his assembled friends (Leverkühn now taking on the mad shape of Hugo Wolf), he tells them how he has been conducting himself during his adult life, he reveals that his whole existence has been phantasmagoric, that he has dwelt among nothing but phantoms and shades.

8

Distance, detachment — *laughter* is also a form of detachment, and irony is, technically speaking, a type of humour. Not to feel pain at something painful, but not even to stand before it in that uncertain and unstable condition called indifference, not merely to feel no pain at the sight of it but to counter the danger of pain with a positive feeling of pleasure — to *laugh* at it: is that not the extremest form of detachment? There is always a kind of smile playing about the lips of him who habitually speaks ironically: sarcasm — irony without nuance — is proverbially the lowest form of humour and will always get a laugh of a harsh and bitter sort. Suppose — to offer an example — one chooses to write about a man who is 'a widower, bereft and forsaken of all the world', so that there is 'not a soul on earth to love him';[74] suppose one adds that the wife of this widower has died in childbirth a short time ago, that the child she bore was born dead, and that the widower has had two previous children but they too are dead; suppose one adds further that the widower has become an alcoholic and as a result has lost his job, so that he has no means of support; and further, that he is extremely ugly and ill-dressed; and suppose then that one sets him on the way to the churchyard to visit 'the graves of his dear departed'.[75] Supposing all this, what would it mean if the story in which he appears is intended to be — a *comic* story? And not merely intended, for *The Way to the*

Churchyard succeeds in being genuinely comic in a funereal sort of way. Or, to put the question differently, what does it mean when the trials and tribulations of Tonio Kröger are made the subject of a comic burlesque, as they are in *Tristan*? My answer is: it means the author has distanced himself so far from the painfulness of what he is describing as to have reached the other end of the emotional spectrum; it means that, in these instances, he has withdrawn his sympathy from his characters so completely he is able to find their miseries and misfortunes funny. If this be true, it will follow that he is likely to find 'humour' in precisely those situations in which, from a conventional point of view, there is *nothing to laugh at*. And that is just where he does find it. With Thomas Mann, humour consists very largely of the narration of unpleasing, uncomfortable, disastrous or conventionally immoral events in such a way as to make them seem to a greater or less degree comic.

To write seriously about humour is to run the risk of being thought humourless. It is a risk I shall have to accept. There is a reason for finding this or that comic; it is not something to be taken for granted. Why, for example, does Mann find the facts recorded in *this* passage funny? 'Bad news came of Christian [Buddenbrook]. His marriage seemed not to have improved his health. He had become more and more subject to uncanny delusions and morbid hallucinations, until finally his wife had acted upon the advice of a physician and had him put into an institution. He was unhappy there, and wrote pathetic letters to his relatives, expressive of a fervent desire to leave the establishment, where, it seemed, he was none too well treated. But they kept him shut up, and it was probably the best thing for him. It also put his wife in a position to continue her former independent existence without prejudice to her status as a married woman or to the practical advantages accruing from her marriage.'[76] The bald facts are rendered humorous by various rhetorical devices: meiosis ('seemed not to have improved his health' for 'made him much more unwell', 'none too well treated' for 'treated abominably'), euphemism ('institution' for 'lunatic asylum', 'former independent status' for 'whoring', 'practical advantages' for 'wealth'), mock pomposity ('expressive of a fervent desire to leave the establishment', 'put his wife in a position', 'without prejudice to'). It goes without saying that the author could, had he been so minded, have rendered the passage quite otherwise; but then he would have read, not like Thomas Mann, but like Strindberg, the trick of whose style consists entirely in the resolute avoidance of irony, understatement and euphemism: 'Christian's marriage made him even madder than he had been before, and his wife finally took the advice of a physician and had him locked up in a lunatic asylum. There he was treated abominably and wrote pathetic letters to his relatives imploring them to have him released. His relatives ignored these appeals because they were glad he was finally out of the way. His wife was now free to resume the life of a whore she had had to abandon when he married her, while at the same time retaining the wealth and respectability she had acquired by marriage.' Why could Mann not write like that, or something like that, if that is what he was trying to tell us? Because, unlike Strindberg, he could not *derive satisfaction* from contemplating the destruction of Christian Buddenbrook and the awfulness of his wife. Christian's fate is, above all, pathetic, and Mann cannot endure to look upon it: consequently, he shields himself from it — with humour.

But it is only humour of a sort, a wry, bitter sort: what about 'genuine' humour, the sort one laughs aloud at? What about *Felix Krull*?

Let us — resolutely braving the possibility of being thought devoid of a sense of humour — investigate the subject of this genuinely comic novel. Felix Krull tells his own story — but that should put us on our guard at the outset. Thomas Mann's normal practice is to tell his stories himself and not to hand over their narration to somebody else. Serenus Zeitblom is the narrator of *Doctor Faustus* only in a very qualified sense: for most of the time Serenus is frankly and (on the 'Leverkühn= Germany' level) formally Thomas Mann himself under an assumed name. 'Clemens the Irishman...from...the cloister of Clonmacnoise'[77] indites the mysterious story of *The Holy Sinner* and constantly reminds us that it is he and no other who is doing so — a practice that has its reasons, which will be gone into in their place, but one which would also be consistent with a certain self-consciousness on the part of the real author, the feeling which might accompany the performance of an unfamiliar role. *The Dilettante* narrates his own comic-pathetic history. But overwhelmingly the voice we hear in Mann's novels and stories is that of Mann himself: he comments continually on the action he is describing, and in *Joseph* he makes no bones about obtruding himself directly into the narrative ('Here it was...I myself went down into the depths and looked...saw all with my own eyes'[78]). Yet throughout this large fragment *Felix Krull*, which would if completed have been a large novel, he gives the telling of the tale wholly over to a voice altogether foreign to his own, one into whose easy-flowing and self-confident discourse his own voice could not obtrude without the greatest incongruity. He has not done this before: why does he do it now? Is it perhaps another instance of 'detachment' — only this time a more complete detachment, a narrative from which the author's voice and views have been completely excluded? For what voice do we hear? One altogether urbane, jocular, untroubled, amused, 'superior'. What is its prevailing tone? Unquestioning, uncritical, unclouded self-approval. What does it speak of? The beauty, genius and worldly success of its truly wonderful possessor, Felix Krull. And what incidents in the life of Felix Krull does it elect to tell us about? Nothing but *conventionally immoral* incidents.

That word immoral suggests, of course, the sexually immoral; but that type of 'immorality' is not what strikes us most forcibly about the immoral nature of Felix Krull's activities. In the moral climate of the 1950s Felix's sexual adventures, such as they are, are not immoral at all, they are merely amusing. The years between *Buddenbrooks* and *The Confessions of Felix Krull* were not *all* bad; on the contrary, one can point to a thousand improvements; and one of them has been the disengagement of sexuality from the realm of morals. Even I, who am only 39 years old, can remember when 'premarital intercourse', as it used revoltingly to be called, was definitely immoral and women especially had to pretend they would no more commit it than they would petty larceny. That, together with the evils to which it gave rise, has now, thank heaven, gone from all centres of enlightenment and we may hope it will be gone altogether before the present decade is at an end. No, Felix's sexual affairs are no longer immoral; and they are to be found in his memoirs only because he thinks they ought to be found there, for among the qualities he fancies he possesses are those of Casanova. What *is* immoral, and what one hopes always will be immoral about his activities is the *petty fraud* they involve.

Petty fraud is Felix Krull's inheritance and the only thing for which he has any real talent. His father's business is the manufacture of a barely drinkable wine impudently labelled '*extra cuvée*'. Felix finds this amusing, and indeed one can imagine worse crimes; but what do we think, in reality, of people who try to sell trash by advertising it as something exceptionally fine? Not that they are terrible criminals, but that they are contemptible: petty fraud is never other than contemptible, it makes one ashamed for the perpetrator. But Felix finds it amusing, admires his father, and is inclined to think the wine business rather ingenious. It becomes the model upon which he patterns his own career. He labels himself '*extra cuvée*' and a number of people are taken in by the label: that, in its essentials, is the career of Felix Krull.

This career, with its perpetual petty deceptions and its occasional stoopings to such vulgar crimes as petty theft, Felix describes with the most self-congratulatory good humour; he is an engaging enough fellow, but it is obvious he has no moral consciousness. He enjoys life (that, really, is why we like him), and he even expresses his approval of life (for which we are grateful), but its total lack of moral values deprives his life of any real value at all. But might this not provide the answer to our question why Thomas Mann chooses to tell the story of this life *in absentia*, to place himself at a two-fold distance from the narrative—firstly by the distancing effect of humour, then by that of the fictional narrator? So that the humour of the novel could be defined as an extreme form of irony: the inversion of the moral judgment of the author (the 'expression of one's meaning by language of opposite...tendency') but with the unspoken but understood true judgment nowhere present? If the life of Felix Krull is without moral content then Mann would, if he was to describe that life, have to employ for the description all the devices of irony at his command: and that means the description would be *comic* and that which is described *unreal*.

That *Felix Krull* is comic needs no proof: just read it. That the world in which he lives is unreal is easy to prove. Felix is a perpetual and hardened liar, and his ideal lie is 'that which in no way deserves to be called deceit, but is the product of a lively imagination which has not yet entered wholly into the realm of the actual'[79]—in other words, he lives in a world which does not exist but might. It is no wonder he describes his life as 'often dreamlike' and his conversation with the prostitute in the cab as possessing 'the free, exalted irresponsibility that is usually a characteristic only of dreams'.[80] This is the true atmosphere of the *Confessions*: that of a dream in which everything comes out well for the dreamer and moral considerations are out of sight. From the beginning of the second part of the novel the progress of the action is determined by chance, sometimes by very uncommon chance: the reappearance of Madame Philibert, from whom Felix has stolen a jewel case, at the hotel at which he works, and his meeting with the wife and daughter of Professor Kuckuck in a Lisbon café are both coincidences so excessively improbable as to give Felix's adventures the air of a happy dream. And it is not irrelevant to notice the reason he gives himself for refusing the tempting offer of Lord Strathbogie: 'The main thing was that a confident instinct within me rebelled against a form of reality that was simply handed to me...rebelled in favour of free play and dreams, self-created and self-sufficient, dependent, that is, only on imagination.'[81] At this time he is living a double life as waiter and dandy-about-town, and between these roles his real existence disappears: 'I masqueraded in both capacities, and...the real I...did not exist.'[82] But this duplicity is as nothing compared with that involved in the masquerade as the Marquis de Venosta: beneath this disguise what is left of reality in Felix Krull disappears and, since the novel breaks off while he is still thus disguised, we never recover him again: he has disappeared into his own dream.

9

Settembrini admonishes Hans Castorp to beware of irony: 'Where irony is not a direct and classic device of oratory, not for a moment equivocal to a healthy mind, it makes for depravity, it becomes a drawback to civilization, an unclean traffic with the forces of reaction, vice, and materialism. As the atmosphere in which we live [i.e. that of a sanatorium] is obviously very favourable to such miasmic growths, I may hope, or rather, I must fear, that you understand my meaning.'[83] We too ought to reflect on the meaning of this admonition—but as we do so we must not forget that it comes to us from *Settembrini*.

5 Myth

What is mythology? It is the manufacture of meaning. At first
there is no meaning and no demand for meaning. A thunderstorm occurs: the animal man notices it but as soon as it is
over he forgets it—a thunderstorm is merely a brute event:
darkness, a flash, a bang. And now it is light and the ground
wet: another brute event. He smells the wet smell. And now
he feels hungry, and eats. One event follows another, each
event 'eternal' while it lasts, life an eternal present. But now an
event occurs which changes the nature of every event that
comes after it: the animal man acquires intelligence, and therewith memory. Henceforth there is no eternal present: every
event is attended by the recollection of those events which it
resembles, as a musical note is attended by its overtones. Now
a thunderstorm is no longer darkness, a flash, a bang. The sky
grows dark, like night; the air grows heavy, like a blanket:
suddenly a huge dagger of light, but more lurid by far than
day, tears through the blackness. It is gone: then the thunder
follows, a roar louder than any animal roar, the loudest of all
sounds. Sometimes the dagger strikes the earth, and burns it;
sometimes it strikes a man, and kills him. *What is it?* What
does it mean when this dagger of light and fire appears in a
sky grown black and the thunder follows? And now there is no
meaning but a demand for meaning.

This demand for meaning, being ultimately a demand that
our fear of that uncanny thing up there shall be ended, is
satisfied when we make it into something familiar, when we
domesticate it, when we say to ourselves: 'that is nothing
uncanny, that is something we have always known all about'.
The *myth* is our explanation to ourselves that what seems non-
human is really human, that what seems coldly incomprehensible really has a quite simple, quite human meaning. And
now we are much less fearful: for that dagger of fire is *only* a
spark from the gods' forge, that thundersound is *only* the crash
of the hammer. Or it is Thor the Hammerer with his hammer:

Thor, whom we also know so much else about—we know that he is a little dense, that the *other* gods and even the giants are able to play tricks on him. And now we are not nearly so afraid of the thunder and lightning; and having explained what *that* is, we can go on and apply our method to everything else. What is the sun, what does the sun mean? The sun is a cart of fire, a blazing cart driven across the sky every day by the Sun-God. And now we know what the sun means. And soon we know what everything means. The world, mankind, life and death: all full, overfull of meaning—a human meaning, it goes without saying, for that is the only meaning we could understand, that is what meaning *means*.

Through the centuries, through the millennia, man has stayed faithful, not to this or that religion, this or that moral code, this or that mode of physical or mental dress, but to this *method of making meaning*, the mythological method. Until, that is, the other day. Driven by whatever urge, mankind the other day turned on his myths and declared—a fateful and perhaps fatal declaration—that they *were not true*. And at once—*meaning* went out of the window. For with the banishment of myth we have banished the meaning made by the myth: and now we no longer have either.

What is the meaning of life? Until the other day that question could have been answered, was answered, the answer seemed obvious, everybody knew it: the meaning of life is that it is a preparation for after-life—everybody knew that. Spenser, for example, knew it:

> And ye high heavens, the temple of the gods,
> In which a thousand torches flaming bright
> Doe burne, that to us wretched earthly clods
> In dreadful darknesse lend desired light
> And all ye powers which in the same remayne,
> More than we men can fayne!
> Poure out your blessing on us plentiously,
> And happy influence upon us raine,
> That we may raise a large posterity,
> Which from the earth, which they may long possesse
> With lasting happinesse,
> Up to your haughty pallaces may mount;
> And, for the guerdon of theyre glorious merit,
> May heavenly tabernacles there inherit,
> Of blessed Saints for to increase the count . . .

Is that not the loveliest expression in English of what life could once mean? Can it mean that now? Is *that* the fate you anticipate for your children? Spenser was in a certain sense a 'religious man', but one had no need to be a religious man to know that the meaning of human life lay in its association with the divine: the fact was accepted *as* a fact everywhere and it is to be discovered everywhere and almost at random. 'There is surely a reason for this want of inborn sympathy between the creature and the creation around it, a reason which may perhaps be found in the widely-differing destinies of man and his earthly sphere. The grandest mountain prospect that the eye can range over is appointed to annihilation. The smallest human interest that the pure heart can feel is appointed to immortality.' These sentiments are to be found in Wilkie Collins's *The Woman in White* and they were published in the same year as *The Origin of Species*, which antiquated them almost before they were written. They now belong to a world which seems a million years gone because the meaning which filled it has gone. You will remember William Blake's question whether the sun was to you a circular object about the size of a guinea or something that declared the glory of God. On television yesterday somebody said the sun is 'actually' a hydrogen-bomb, and clearly he did not suppose he was saying anything very startling. Now *we* know that the sun is 'actually' not a hydrogen-bomb, or a blazing cart, or something the size of a guinea, or something that declares the glory of God: *actually* the sun is a star. What is a star? The Middle Ages knew that a star is a hole in the floor of Heaven: that was the meaning of a star—and in that sense we no longer know *what* a star is, our knowledge of the nature of a star is only a piece of information, not 'meaning'. In the sense that the ancients knew that the sun is a blazing cart, in the sense that Blake knew it was something that declared the glory of God, we no longer know *what* the sun is. As to primitive man, pre-myth man, so to us the sun is merely a *brute fact*. And the earth and the sea, the thunder, the seasons, life, death, mankind: all again brute facts, things that merely *are*, things without meaning.

Now again there is no meaning but a demand for meaning: and this demand has produced solutions which are certainly very strange and ingenious, not to say 'modern', but none of which has up till now proved satisfactory. It has been suggested to us that an *absence of meaning* can itself be a meaning — a suggestion which is unfortunately at bottom no more than a play on words. It has been suggested that life is 'absurd' and man 'a useless passion' — but life cannot be nourished and fortified by insipid food of this sort. It has been suggested that to speak of a 'meaning of life' at all is to speak meaninglessly and that we had better disregard the question and get on quietly with something more modest — advice which, however well meant, comes 20,000 years too late. When we lost religion we still had philosophy, and we hoped to recover from philosophy what our loss of religion had taken away: but, instead of that happening, we have only lost philosophy as well. 'Existentialism' and 'positivism' — if one is still entitled to use those labels — are products, not of philosophy, but of the breakdown of philosophy: they show what happens when the synthesis of ethics and epistemology which is what has been meant by philosophy since the time of Plato proves unstable and falls apart.

There has been a big attempt to endow a philosophy with the pathos of religion, an attempt corresponding, within the breakdown of our own civilization, to the Stoic reaction to the breakdown of classical civilization. Like Stoicism, Communism is a noble ethical doctrine founded on an improbable metaphysic which, if taken seriously, undermines it. The metaphysic of 'dialectical materialism' is that there is no metaphysical world yet the physical world, which is all there is, follows metaphysical laws: this is unlikely and mere slovenly thinking prompted by self-interest. 'The laws of history' — but when you give up God ('the metaphysical world') you give up 'law', that much should be clear at the outset. The 'laws of history', like the Stoics' 'necessity', is superstition.

These have all been attempts to push forward, to answer loss of meaning with the discovery of new meaning; but the reverse, the move backwards, *atavism*, was also to be expected and has in fact occurred. The Japanese, a people upon whom civilization, their own included, has always sat very lightly (a fact to which their punctilious observation of its forms bears witness) slipped down to an extreme depth of primitivism as soon as the occasion offered itself. Compulsions which might have been thought extinct in man were shown to be still very lively in the Japanese, and pose the question how it is possible for a race to be technologically gifted and socially sophisticated almost beyond any other and at the same time morally and emotionally the most primitive race on earth. Japanese 'war criminals' were not Westerners who had gone wrong, but men whose norms of reference were different and whose behaviour was thus different and could involve enormous and casual massacre, genocide, routine torture, the starvation, mistreatment and murder of prisoners as a matter of course, cannibalism, ceremonial beheading with the sword, and suicide as a means of combat, all without the slightest trace of bad conscience. Such modes of behaviour belong to a very early level of civilization: even when the Greeks of the city state era sometimes attempted the genocide of those they had defeated it was a case of atavism. On this level, 'thinking' is entirely a matter of the weaving of myths and fantasies, and it would have been incredible if the atavistic behaviour of the Japanese had not been accompanied by an equivalent *mental* regression. And it was so accompanied: the form of the Japanese state was so regressive that one has to go back to Egypt or the Aztec empire before one meets it again: the Emperor as Sun-God! The West found this conception so impossible to believe it refused to believe the Japanese themselves could really believe it: but that they did really believe it their behaviour bears witness. If one's conduct is that of the age of mythology, one's mental make-up is likely to be that of the age of mythology too.

This was one nation that regressed to mythology and thereby propagated a nightmare. Another was the German. But here the pathos was quite different. Bad conscience assumed among the Germans the proportions of an epidemic and led to a national amnesia. (' "I have done that", says my memory. "I cannot have done that" — says my pride, and remains adamant. At last — memory yields' (*Nietzsche*[1]).) Everything Nazi vanished: that was the first effect of defeat — vanished from the home, vanished from the street, vanished from the map, vanished from the mind. 'I did not know what was going on', that much-ridiculed plea, was often, of course, a lie: but even more often it was a way of saying 'I *cannot remember* what was going on.' For what was the Nazi era? It was that era in German history in which all the worst fears of what would happen when the values of the Christianized West fell away were realized and *exceeded*. That the Germans would revert to pre-Christian mythology as soon as the Christian had lost its hold, that the German Revolution, when it came, would be atavistic, had been prophesied long before the thing happened. It was prophesied, for example, by Heine, who declared that German philosophy, preceding the German Revolution, would only make that revolution all the more dreadful. 'Through these doctrines,' he said, 'there have evolved revolutionary forces that only await the day when they can break out and fill the world with horror and amazement'; and the worst will be effected by the adherent of the German 'philosophy of nature' who 'enters into an alliance with the primaeval forces of nature' and 'can conjure the daemonic forces of old-Germanic pantheism', so that 'there awakens within him that belligerency [*Kampflust*] which we find in the ancient Germans...Christianity ...to some extent assuaged that brutal Germanic *Kampflust*, but could not eradicate it, and if one day that restraining talisman, the Cross, should collapse, then the savagery of the ancient warriors, the mad berserker rage,...will come rattling up again. That talisman is decaying and the day will come when it will fall miserably to pieces. Then the old stone gods will rise up out of the long-forgotten ruins and rub the thousand-year dust from their eyes, and Thor with his giant hammer will at last leap up and shatter the Gothic cathedrals.' When that happens, says Heine, 'a piece will be played in Germany compared with which the French Revolution may well look like a harmless idyll'.[2]

This prophesy, which has become quite famous since it was fulfilled, was, so to speak, *over*-fulfilled: the meaning of life went, not only in the general sense we have been describing, but in a more violent and palpable sense: in Germany it was *stamped out*, and for millions of men ordinary existence had simply no meaning at all. Into this vacuum came the myth: the pre-Christian myth of race-virtue, blood-virtue, election by courage; the pre-scientific myth of racial purity (the *pure* races are, by a well-understood biological necessity, extinct); the myth that the Germanic peoples were *hard* (the Romans were much harder, the antique nations, the Assyrians for example, incomparably harder—the Germans were merely boisterous); the myth of *Treue*, the Nibelungen-virtue: in short, a pagan mythology designed to bestow meaning on life and in particular to endow *German* life, the fact of one's being German, with a special, a supreme meaning—a meaning that would again make life worthwhile.

The Nazi *Weltanschauung* was a highly selective revival of primitive myths blended with modern and mistaken notions of what the primitive Germans were like. Intellectually it is nonsense and, but for a consideration to be gone into in our last chapter, one would fall into despair to think it was produced by the best-educated nation in Europe, the nation most habituated to philosophical thinking. As a historical phenomenon, however, it is, for precisely that reason, something impossible to neglect. It shows how, after every rational and philosophical idea currently available had failed to supply final or even provisional truth, the kind of mind most conversant with these ideas turned away from them and towards *mythology* again. Or—in terms of our own subject, to which this disquisition on myth and meaning now leads us back—how much in tune with the age it was that *The Magic Mountain* should have been followed by *Joseph and his Brothers*.

2

The 'philosophies' by which Europe had tried and was still trying to live had, at Haus Berghof, come to nothing; and from this self-destructive play of ideas Mann turned, as if weary of describing only decline and confusion, to a *cheerful myth*. Germany, after its philosophy had failed it, sought meaning in mythology; Thomas Mann did so too.

This huge mythological novel *Joseph and his Brothers*, which occupied Mann for sixteen years, explains itself over and over again: far from posing as the inventor of the story he is telling, the author speaks as if he were a lecturer addressing a class. It is a tone unlike that of any other novel I have read. The reader is assumed throughout to be completely familiar with the Genesis story of Jacob and his sons: the author's self-imposed task is to elucidate it. The elucidation is so extensive one might suppose that nothing was left unexplained, that the author had forestalled any commentator. Yet, in all this mass of explanation and commentary, he nowhere answers in plain words the two questions which loom largest and which, considering the way in which the novel is written, might have been answered most clearly: what myth? and why Joseph?

What myth?—that is to say, what is the meaning imposed on the events described? Why Joseph?—that is to say, what attracted Mann to precisely this legendary figure and his history?

The answer to the second question will help towards answering the first. One of the earliest descriptions of Joseph depicts in the following way his relation to his father Jacob and his mother Rachel: 'Disquiet, questioning, hearkening and seeking, wrestling for God, a bitterly sceptical labouring over the true and the just, the whence and the whither, his own name, his own nature, the true meaning of the Highest—how all that... found expression in Jacob's look, in his lofty brow and the peering, careworn gaze of his brown eyes; and how confidingly Joseph loved this nature, of which his own was aware as a nobility and a distinction and which, precisely as a consciousness of higher concerns and anxieties, lent to his father's person all the dignity, reserve and solemnity which made it so impressive. Unrest and dignity—that is the sign of the spirit; and with childishly unabashed fondness Joseph recognized the seal of tradition upon his father's brow, so different from that upon his own, which was so much blither and freer, coming as it chiefly did from his lovely mother's side, and making him the conversable, social, communicable being he pre-eminently was.'[3] These words have a familiar sound: they remind us of these other, far more familiar words:

> Vom Vater hab ich die Statur,
> Des Lebens ernstes Führen,
> Vom Mütterlein die Frohnatur
> Und Lust zu fabulieren.

Is Joseph 'the artist' in yet another manifestation—Thomas Mann, with his earnest father and artistic mother, disguised as a Biblical hero? Once we have come to suspect it, evidence begins to flood in from all sides. Joseph's relationship with his brothers is, in a very heavily emphasized fashion, that of the artist-outsider with society: it is the old antithesis of artist and bourgeois, genius and commonplace, disguised in old-world garments and old-world phraseology. When we first catch sight of him, Joseph is worshipping the moon, a practice described by the author as 'somewhat decadent', and Gad's description of him as 'little fop and harlot'[4] is not altogether unjustified.

From the point of view of his brothers, his most annoying and unsettling characteristic is that he is a compulsive tale-bearer and even tale-inventor, and it is remarked that he can write while they cannot. All these things suggest the artist in his role as a source of irritation to the society in which he lives. But the worst thing about Joseph is his visions and the naive egoism of which they are an expression. The dream of the sheaves and the dream of the sun, moon and stars infuriate his brothers; if he had told them the dream of being taken up to heaven they would probably have blown their minds even without the stimulus of the coat of many colours, the visible symbol of Joseph's election. His brothers cannot endure Joseph because he is their superior and cannot help revealing the fact. This sense of superiority is something that never deserts him, even after his 'death and rebirth': together with his artist's eloquence and acquaintanceship with dreams, this is his abiding characteristic. 'Already he was no longer the least of these here below; already there were those who bowed before his steps' after he had been appointed assistant to Potiphar's steward. 'But there must be much more than this; for the sake of his God he was filled with the idea that not some but all must bow—all, with the exception of One, the Highest, whom alone he might serve. Such was now the fixed and unchanging principle which guided the life of the descendant of Abram.'[5] But it always had been the fixed principle which guided his life: and although, while in the pit into which his brothers had thrown him, he had come to recognize the naivety of his egoism and to call it 'self-destructive arrogance',[6] he never puts it off. It is the arrogance of Tonio Kröger, of Adrian Leverkühn, even of Felix Krull: the arrogance of conscious superiority.

In all these respects Joseph is a typical Mann artist-nature— but in one respect he differs from all the others except the parodistic Felix: he knows he is inevitably destined for victory. The agonizings of Tonio, Adrian's devil-pact, the despairings of Gregory, are not for him: he is born 'chosen', he inherits 'the blessing' and he lives blithely on in the consciousness that, whatever accidents may befall him, he must in the long run come out on top. Even at the bottom of the pit he experiences no doubts on this head: he merely comes to think he has mis-judged the speed of his success because he has underrated—or perhaps failed to take into account at all—the effect his evident superiority and self-confidence would have on other people. As a result of this experience he learns to exercise a degree of cunning and concealment; and thereafter he never suffers a comparable reverse again. When he is sent down into the pit a second time — his removal to prison at the instance of Potiphar's wife — his mood is one of perfect composure: he knows quite well that nothing can really harm him. For this reason — and herein lies the key to him — he is irrepressibly cheerful, and thus the whole book too is cheerful.

Joseph, 'the man of the blessing', is the light side of Mynheer Peeperkorn, just as Cipolla had been his dark side: the self-sufficient force of personality which on the magic mountain was able effortlessly to dominate exhausted reason and virtue and for a time to raise the other inhabitants of that domain above their normal level of existence. As such, he is the type of mythological hero understood today by the term 'superman': the genius of light to whom everything is easy. It is a myth which received great impetus from Nietzsche, although he, of course, did not invent it, and his 'superman' is a precisely defined conception differing in essential respects from the popular idea of it. Joseph resembles Nietzsche's superman only in so far as he resembles Goethe — a point we shall come to in a moment. As an individual his 'herodom' consists in his being an instrument of the Divine Purpose: it is this which ensures his eventual triumph. God is a major personage in the novel, but he is not recognizably the God of any known religion: perhaps he resembles the Lord of the Book of Job and thus the Lord of the prologue to *Faust*, who is modelled on him, more than he does any other God; but his relationship with the Heavenly Host and with mankind is so peculiar and, in the last resort, so lacking in anything 'godlike', that one is driven into regarding him as an intellectual construct put together by a very ingenious mind which is seeking to reconcile and represent contemporaneously in one person the differing, conflicting and evolving ideas of God present in Biblical and Egyptian mythology. Since his author also introduces the idea of evolution itself into him, so that, in addition to being an amalgam of differing conceptions of godhead, he is also and at the same time evolving into the God of Abraham, Isaac and Jacob; and since it is in addition suggested that these human actors are in some sense the creators of the God they subsequently worship, who, after they have created him, assumes discrete existence—I leave it to you how much credibility is left to him. As theology the novel is fantasy and phantasmagoria; and what 'purpose' this literally unbelievable divinity is working out through his 'Chosen Seed' I, at any rate, am unable to reveal. But does that matter? Only in so far as the elaborate but in the end unconvincing mythological machinery serves to obscure the actual myth. 'Divine Purpose' can here only be the mode in which the hero, the 'superman', expresses to himself his sense of invincibility. Of any coherent, comprehensible 'purpose' in God's behaviour there is not the remotest sign; God himself is neither coherent nor comprehensible; what *is* clear, comprehensible and consistent is the hero's sureness of step and certainty of victory, his inner poise, the security and infallibility of his instincts, and, as a consequence of this, his enjoyment of existence. Joseph's *cheerfulness* is the key to his conception of Divine Purpose: he trusts in the goodness of God, and believes he is chosen by God, because he feels happy on earth—he explains his happiness by a myth. This method of explanation is, of course, the one adopted throughout the Old Testament: when the nation prospers, it means God is pleased; when the nation suffers, it means God is displeased. That is how the Jews gave meaning to their prospering and suffering; and this, in a novel which ransacks Old Testament myth for both its machinery and its meaning, is how the hero gives meaning to his state of permanent well-being. The myth of *Joseph and his Brothers*—the meaning manufactured by that novel—is the myth of Divine Purpose; the brute fact which the myth seeks to give meaning to is the hero's cheerful invincibility. Joseph, as Mann discovered and interpreted him, is the artist happy and victorious; the huge dramatized lecture in which the story of Joseph is simultaneously unfolded and commented on, is a celebration and explanation of this state of being.

3

Mann interrupted *Joseph* to write *Lotte in Weimar*. Let us not forget that this is just as much a work of imagination as *Joseph*. Indeed, the technique is all but identical: documents are ransacked for material out of which a grand central figure is constructed. It is superbly done: but since Thomas Mann cannot really have known what was going on in the brain of Goethe on a certain morning more than a hundred years previously, the resulting portrait of that great man is necessarily a subjective one. This may sound obvious, but it is easily forgotten. We commonly speak of a 'literary portrait', and in the case of *Lotte* the expression is unavoidable: but we also commonly forget that this is a metaphor. A word-picture of a man, unless it is confined to a simple description of his physical appearance, can never be objective in the way a painted portrait is bound to be no matter how much imagination has gone into its creation. It must, at the very least, be interpretation, and very often it will be something altogether imaginative: a portrait as the author sees it but as perhaps no one else sees it. Whether this portrait is found convincing or unconvincing will, within wide bounds, again be a subjective matter. The objective fact—the gentleman's face—is precisely what is *not* available to the literary portraitist: *he* wants to look into the gentleman's soul, and that is, objectively, not to be seen: its existence and nature have to be interpreted from documents which, however much of 'soul' they may contain, are not themselves soul. In the sense in which Mr Gladstone (was it?) said the camera could not lie, the literary camera cannot do anything *but* lie—more precisely, we can never know it is not lying.

The portrait of Goethe the production of which is virtually the whole purpose of *Lotte in Weimar* is deeply considered and very persuasive: it is a real-seeming figure, if a complex one. Five characteristics predominate.

First, Goethe is, both instinctively and intentionally, ambiguous: he is capable of a very great range of moods, but none of them is basic, none is 'really' him. What is 'really' him is precisely this ambiguity and all-sidedness. The mode in which he expresses to himself his freedom from compulsion to assume any one fixed attitude towards life is that of a conscious desire for 'wholeness', for experiencing the totality of things. In his internal monologue of chapter seven, he asserts that the universe is 'all one', and that 'only he who had unity' could 'understand it'.[7] Language of this sort must not be allowed to mislead us: we must grasp what is meant by a 'unity' such as is spoken of here: it means the opposite of a unity, being not one thing but everything. The paradox is only verbal but none the less capable of causing all manner of confusion, and we would do well to get free of it once and for all. It derives from Hegel's peculiar adaptation of Kant's classification of the categories of reason. There are, you will remember, twelve categories, arranged in four groups of three: the categories of quantity, of quality, of relation, and of modality; and Kant observes that the third category in each group arises from a connexion of the first and second of its group. The categories of quantity are unity, plurality and totality, and the category totality arises from a connexion of unity and plurality, being plurality regarded as unity. This is the origin of Hegel's 'dialectic', and the way in which Hegel proceeds, and especially the terminology he insists on using, gives rise to paradoxes which can be resolved by referring back to their Kantian origin. In this instance, the paradox comes merely from using the word 'unity' (the first category of quantity) when what is meant is 'totality' (the third category of quantity): such a usage produces the illusion that when one says that the universe is 'a unity', or when Mann's Goethe says that 'only he who had unity' could understand the universe, one is saying something different from, and much more significant than that the universe is the totality of everything and that only he who had the totality of everything in him could comprehend the universe. The former observation sounds remarkably profound and mystical, the latter is merely an obvious truism: but the former *means* the latter, and nothing more—a fact which would itself be obvious but for the misuse of words. (A worse evil, to consider which would take us too far from our subject, is that one not only *says* 'unity' but *believes in* 'unity', one believes that the totality of everything is in some sense more than a 'mere' totality, that it is informed by some unifying principle—and this without any evidence except a terminological error which probably originates in a *desire* to be misled in this way.)

Mann's Goethe, then, uses the word unity when he means totality: he wants to be all-sided, to experience and contain everything. He has the idea of writing the history of the Cosmos, and asks himself: 'Who can do it, if not I?'[8] He refuses to take sides against one part of life on behalf of another part, he wants to 'accept, to refer, relate, to be the whole, to shame the partisans of every principle by rounding it out — and the other side too'.[9] He says that 'life could not be borne unless we glozed it over with warm, deceptive feeling', and that beneath feeling there always lies 'the icy coldness' of truth:[10] but he does not, on account of that insight, reject feeling or reject truth: he desires both. He says that 'cruelty is one of the chief ingredients of love...What if sweet love itself were put together out of nothing but sheer horrors and the very purest just a compound of shadinesses we dare not confess to!'[11] — an instance of the opposition of feeling and the icy truth behind it: but he rejects neither love nor truth. He says of himself that he has 'never heard of a crime I could not have committed',[12] but he does not despise himself on that account: on the contrary, it is just this capacity for the worst which he thinks a precondition for the highest achievement: 'the depths must laugh!' he exclaims. 'Profundity must smile', and he proposes to himself an art 'that utters shameless things with utter dignity, resolves the hardest riddles with an easy jest'.[13]

All this belongs to his private nature, a nature into which his contemporaries are granted only the rarest glimpse. Its outward and public effect is one of ambiguity, of ironic indifference and detachment, and of moral uncertainty. This last is the second predominating characteristic of the portrait. Goethe is mentioned as accidentally encountering his son with the wife of a hussar and withdrawing with the words 'Children, don't disturb yourselves'.[14] The narrator of the incident refrains from passing comment, but it is clear that it is supposed to display Goethe's moral laxity; and he is, in fact, regarded by his entourage as a man of very accommodating moral principles. In his conversation with Lotte, August Goethe says that people found *Wilhelm Meister* 'a mass of pornography', the *Roman Elegies* 'a sink of iniquity', *The God and the Bayadere* and *The Bride of Corinth* 'priapic indecency', and *Elective Affinities* 'lascivious'.[15] These judgments are baffling now, and Goethe's son is not presented as agreeing with them: but we who read the novel are, perhaps, expected to see in them some tincture of truth: Goethe is, by the standards of his age, unconventional: he is morally out of tune with his time.

The third main characteristic is that he is wholly out of sympathy with the political aspirations of his country. Referring to the War of Liberation, he says: 'I stood calmly and let the raging storm pass over my head';[16] and it is said of him that he 'utterly failed...to share the new patriotic life of the German people' and compelled his son to 'remain aloof'.[17] This attitude of disdain for the forces of liberation from Napoleon has, since the war ended, passed over into something like disdain for the German people as such. He prophesies that the 'crassest follies' will be displayed by the Germans as a consequence of their new-found love of fatherland;[18] he says of them that they 'hate clarity' and 'love cloudy vapouring and berserker excesses', that they 'abandon themselves credulously to every fanatic scoundrel who speaks to their baser qualities, confirms them in their vices, teaches them that nationality means barbarism and isolation', and that they think themselves great 'only when they have gambled away all that they had worth having';[19] and he accuses them of a 'pig-headed craving to be a unique nation', which he calls a 'national narcissism that wants to make its own stupidity a pattern and power over the rest of the world!'[20] 'Unhappy folk!' he exclaims. 'They will end in a smash'.[21]

Fourthly, he is a burden on and in some sense a danger to the circle around him. During the long dinner party at which Lotte meets him again and discovers she no longer likes him very much, Goethe says the Chinese had a saying that 'the great man is a national misfortune'.[22] This remark is not explained, but Lotte feels that in some way it is true, and that it applies to Goethe. He himself is constrained to admit—publicly and not, as earlier, simply to himself—that it seemed always to have been his fate 'to involve myself innocently in guilt',[23] and Lotte does not contradict him, except perhaps to question the entire appropriateness of that 'innocently': on the contrary, she says that his circle looks 'almost like a battlefield and the kingdom of a wicked emperor'.[24]

Lastly, Thomas Mann's Goethe finds everything easy. This is the quality about him which, in the final resort, impresses his disciples most immediately and continually, and for the sake of which they forgive him for being what he is in other respects. Everyone who speaks of him remarks on the astonishing combination in him of versatility and the highest excellence: he seems, although he is not, a universal genius, a man who can do anything better than anyone else, and do it easily. This quality had already been remarked on long before by Schiller, in the story *A Weary Hour*; labouring at his desk, Schiller thinks of that other man over in Weimar, 'that radiant being, so sense-endowed, so divinely unconscious', whom he calls 'an effortless and gushing spring'.[25]

Now, these five qualities in combination produce a figure which, whether or not it resembles the historical Goethe, certainly resembles very closely the Goethe imagined by Nietzsche: '*Goethe*—not a German event but a European one: a grand attempt to overcome the eighteenth century through a return to nature, through a going-*up* to the naturalness of the Renaissance, a kind of self-overcoming on the part of that century. He bore within him its strongest instincts: sentimentality, nature-idolatry, the anti-historical, the idealistic, the unreal and revolutionary...He called to his aid history, the natural sciences, antiquity, likewise Spinoza, above all practical activity; he surrounded himself with nothing but closed horizons; he did not sever himself from life, he placed himself within it; nothing could discourage him and he took as much as possible upon himself, above himself, within himself. What he aspired to was *totality*; he strove against the separation of reason, sensuality, feeling, will...he disciplined himself to a whole, he *created* himself...Goethe was, in an era disposed to the unreal, a convinced realist: he affirmed everything which was related to him in this respect—he had no greater experience than that *ens realissimum* called Napoleon. Goethe conceived of a strong, highly cultured human being, skilled in all physical accomplishments, who, keeping himself in check and having reverence for himself, dares to allow himself the whole compass and wealth of naturalness, who is strong enough for this freedom; a man of tolerance, not out of weakness, but out of strength, because he knows how to employ to his advantage what would destroy an average nature; a man to whom nothing is forbidden, except it be *weakness*, whether that weakness be called vice or virtue.'[26]

The lineaments of Mann's Goethe can, I think, be seen again in this other word-picture: the all-sidedness, the moral ambiguity, the admiration for Napoleon. Nietzsche elsewhere celebrates, and probably exaggerates, Goethe's anti-Germanism: 'Goethe's heart opened up at the phenomenon Napoleon—it *closed* up to the "Wars of Liberation"', he writes,[27] and quotes with approval Goethe's words to Eckermann: 'We Germans are but of yesterday. To be sure, we have for a century been acquiring culture very successfully, only it may take another couple of centuries before sufficient spirit and higher culture penetrates our compatriots and becomes general among them for it to be possible to say of them that it is a long time *since they were barbarians.*'[28] And the 'Chinese proverb' which Lotte applies to Goethe himself is also to be discovered in Nietzsche: 'The *danger* which lies in great human beings...is extraordinary; sterility, exhaustion of every kind follow in their footsteps. The great human being is a terminus.'[29] But where this conception of Goethe leads to—its real significance for Nietzsche—is to be seen in the words which follow the above-quoted description: 'A spirit thus *emancipated* stands in the midst of the universe with a joyful and trusting fatalism, in the *faith* that only what is separate and individual may be rejected, that in the totality everything is redeemed and affirmed—*he no longer denies*...But such a faith is the highest of all possible faiths: I have baptised it with the name *Dionysus.*'[30] During the course of Nietzsche's works the meaning of the name Dionysus changes. We have seen already what it means in *The Birth of Tragedy*: the basic drives brought under control by the form-creating force, Apollo. Subsequently, however, Nietzsche came to think this dualistic idea unwarrantable: the basic drives must somehow bestow form on themselves. From this there arose his conception of sublimation or self-overcoming; and when he had reduced the remaining multiplicity of drives to a single drive, which he called will to power, he was left with the monistic conception of sublimated will to power as the form-giving force: to this phenomenon he then transferred the name Dionysus, who is now the former Dionysus plus the former Apollo. In Nietzsche's later works, the 'Dionysian man' is the 'self-overcome' man or 'superman': and his description of Goethe in fact defines what he means by 'superman' more concisely than any other passage in his works.

Nietzsche's Goethe is a model of the superman; and, in so far as Mann's Goethe takes after him, so is he. The figure presented in *Lotte in Weimar* is thus a variant of the mythological hero depicted in *Joseph and his Brothers*: the genius to whom everything comes easily, the 'superman' whose existence is a kind of justification of existence in general, a meaning bestowed on life. The milieu is, of course, totally different; and there is no question of finding rigid correspondence of detail — in *Lotte*, for example, there is nothing corresponding to the Divine Purpose of *Joseph*. But both works clearly reflect an identical attitude of mind — a fact not in itself surprising, since they are exact contemporaries: it is the attitude of a mind which has ceased to place reliance on philosophical ideas, and has turned to the myth of the 'man of the blessing'. Goethe holding court at the dinner table, eating and drinking to excess but without any ill effect, effortlessly dominating his circle, is Mynheer Peeperkorn once more.

But he is also — so obviously the fact is likely to escape attention — 'the artist', indeed the supreme artist among Mann's artist-figures. And for once, both historically and in the context of Mann's fiction, the artist and the bourgeois are reconciled in him: he is both, there is no conflict between them, they coexist as opposite poles of that 'whole' which Goethe tries to be. Rightly considered, the union of artist and bourgeois in Goethe is the high point of Mann's optimistic phase, the era of his life when he determined, so far as his creative work was concerned, to believe in the possibility that all the former conflicts and antitheses might be resolved by the existence and agency of the 'superman', the self-justified, integrated and integrating personality; and when he resumed *Joseph* it was no more than natural that he should go on to celebrate the redemption of an entire society by the patient activity of the man of the blessing. Joseph 'the Provider' is the anti-Cipolla: the *light* side of Peeperkorn become charismatic leader. And with that consummation, the myth of *Joseph and his Brothers* is seen to be the specific *counter-myth* to the Nazi myth: an attempt, not to argue against that which is impervious to argument, but to set up, with conscious historical intention, an opposing myth. The admiration for the magnetic personality which had, against the author's will, made itself evident in *Mario and the Magician*, can here flourish openly with a good conscience. The work in which it does so, the largest and most elaborate work of the greatest German writer of his age, can stand over against the work going forward in Germany while it was being written, and may one day be thought to have redeemed that era of German history from utter infamy.

6 Crime

Joseph was Thomas Mann's ark: when the fountains of the great deep were broken up he climbed aboard and stayed aloft. But when the flood began to subside the stench of drowned cities reached up even into the ark; and as soon as there was dry land again he left the ark and went down deeper into the drowned world than he had ever been before, drawn by a desire to see the extent of the havoc. And then back it all comes, the badness, the rottenness, the darkness, the unreality and meaninglessness: it had been there all the time, only submerged. Here, for example, is something that seemed to have been overcome and abolished but was merely submerged. The Devil addresses Adrian Leverkühn: 'Do you believe in anything like an *ingenium* that has nothing to do with hell? *Non datur*! The artist is the brother of the criminal and the madman. Do you ween that any important work was ever wrought except its maker learned to understand the way of the criminal and madman?'[1] The reconciliation of the artist and the bourgeois in Goethe as a single, self-justifying personality is undone again in the revival of the idea that the artist is a criminal—not in the sense in which Goethe declared himself capable of any crime (this is simply a consequence of his 'wholeness', of his containing both sides), but in that of the preponderance in the artist of anti-social instincts.

And so we are back in the cruel world of nihilist Europe, where such an event as that recorded in *Little Lizzie* seems to be quite in order and almost normal. There is a lawyer called Jacoby who is married to a woman the initials of whose names spell the word Amra, which is the name she is known by. Her colouring is that of the 'dull, dark sallowness of the south' and she has 'artless brown eyes'—we have met her before, certainly. Jacoby is grotesquely fat, 'a perfect colossus of a man',[2] he resembles an elephant. Like Tobias Mindernickel, he suffers from a deficiency of self-assertion and seems always to be apologizing for his existence. He is in a continual agony of apprehension lest his wife betray him; and his fears are well grounded, since she has already done so with 'a gifted young musician' named Alfred Läutner, for whom she is 'on fire with guilty passion'.[3] One spring, Amra has the notion of celebrating the new beer—all this is taking place in gay Bavaria—by holding a big beer party. She and her friends get together to plan an entertainment, as the climax of which, Amra suggests, Jacoby shall appear 'as a *chanteuse*, in a red satin baby frock, and do a dance'.[4] Later she proposes he shall sing as well, and that Alfred Läutner shall compose a song for the occasion. Jacoby refuses, then agrees. Subsequently Amra has the further inspiration that Läutner shall compose the accompaniment to the song and dance for four hands, so that he and she can sit side by side and play while Jacoby performs. And so it happens: Jacoby, dressed as a woman, sings and dances while his wife and her lover accompany him at the piano. The act is not amusing: 'Horror was in the depths of all these spellbound eyes, gazing at this pair and at that husband there. The monstrous, unspeakable scandal lasted five long minutes',[5] at the end of which time Jacoby breaks into the song 'Little Lizzie' which Läutner has composed. In the middle of it awareness of the situation suddenly floods over him and he falls dead with the shock.

This ghastly tale, which belongs within the ambit of *Professor Unrat* and marks the closest approach of Thomas Mann to Heinrich Mann, would be of slight interest were it not for the presence in it of Herr Alfred Läutner. The author goes to some pains to persuade us that Herr Läutner is a genuine artist: 'He belonged to the present-day race of small artists, who do not demand the utmost of themselves, whose first requirement is to be jolly and happy, who employ their pleasing little talents to heighten their personal charms', but he has a touch of something more about him: he 'wrote pretty things, mostly waltzes and mazurkas. They would have been rather too gay and popular to be considered music as I understand it, if each of them had not contained a passage of some originality, a modulation, a harmonic phrasing, some sort of bold effect that betrayed wit and invention, which was evidently the point of the whole and which made it interesting to genuine musicians.'[6] The 'bold effect' which gives life to the song 'Little Lizzie' is described as 'an inspiration which was almost a stroke of genius', a 'sudden phrase of genuine creative art'.[7] On a small scale and in a minor way, Herr Läutner is a real artist. He is also 'entirely unmoral and unscrupulous', has 'not enough more fibre' to resist Amra's seductions,[8] and after only the briefest hesitation becomes violently enthusiastic at the idea of composing a song for Jacoby to sing and dance to. It would place too great a strain on this character to describe him as an artist who is also a criminal: but the egg is there, the creativity combined with total lack of moral scruple that will in the end be hatched and grow into another composer who will play fourhanded, not with his neighbour's wife, but with the Devil.

2

'Listen to this. I know a banker...who has a gift for writing stories. He employs this gift in his idle hours, and some of his stories are of the first rank. But despite...this excellent gift... he has had to serve a prison sentence, on anything but trifling grounds. Yes, it was actually first *in prison* that he became conscious of his gift, and his experiences as a convict are the main theme in all his works. One might be rash enough to conclude that a man has to be at home in some kind of jail in order to become a poet. But can you escape the suspicion that the source and essence of his being an artist had less to do with his life in prison than they had with the reasons that *brought him there*?'[9] Thus Tonio Kröger (italics his). Tonio believes that the artist is a criminal in the most literal sense: a man whose instincts are of the sort that might land him in prison. Later on he is, in a famous incident, confirmed in his opinion when he himself is nearly arrested. The scene is of the highest interest. Tonio has returned to his native town from Munich on his way to Denmark, but the place seems utterly unreal to him, he has altogether lost touch with it. As he is about to leave his hotel he is stopped by the proprietor, who has a policeman with him. The police are looking out for a fugitive whose description might fit Tonio Kröger. Tonio has difficulty in proving his identity, and is embarrassed at having to declare his name and occupation. His embarrassment seems to confirm the policeman's suspicions: ' "Hm," said the policeman. "And you give out that you are not identical with an individdle named" — he said "individdle" and then, referring to his document in coloured inks, spelled out an involved, fantastic name which mingled all the sounds of all the races—Tonio Kröger forgot it the next minute—"of unknown parentage and unspecified means," he went on, "wanted by the Munich police for various shady transactions, and probably in flight towards Denmark?" '10 The entire episode of Tonio's return home is phantasmagoric, but this scene is dreamlike in a literal sense—I mean it might have been transcribed from an actual dream. The description of the fugitive is in fact a description of Tonio Kröger as he believes himself to be; and the name the policeman says which mingles names of differing racial origin and which Tonio immediately forgets is, of course, his own name. 'It is only a formality', says the proprietor in an effort to smooth things over; and that, indeed, is what the incident is: Tonio's formal confession to the police that he is a criminal.

That deceit is the artist's normal occupation is asserted with even less circumspection in *The Infant Prodigy*. Bibi Saccellaphylaccas, the boy pianist, possesses 'the most harmless childish countenance in the world'.[11] This countenance is a fraud. He is eight years old but given out for seven; his dress suggests an innocence which its wearer does not possess; the programme notes for his recital are humbug; he begins his act, as it may rightly be called, with a gesture which the author insists is insincere; and when he takes his bow his thoughts contradict his actions. Bibi is altogether bogus: and his case is generalized when, at the conclusion of his recital, a 'girl with untidy hair and swinging arms' confesses to herself: 'We are all infant prodigies, we artists.'[12]

Here is Bibi at the piano: 'He sat and played, so little, so white and shining, against the great black grand piano, elect and alone, above that confused sea of faces, above the heavy, insensitive mass soul, upon which he was labouring to work with his individual, differentiated soul.'[13] We shall shortly meet the great Müller-Rosé, the most cruelly exposed artist in Thomas Mann's whole menagerie of artists and thus a key figure for an understanding of the rest: when we do, we ought to remember the boy pianist at work on the 'mass soul' of his audience and realize what sinister depths the author wants us to glimpse even here, within this diminutive child artist.

If Tonio Kröger and Bibi Saccellaphylaccas are criminals, it would be surprising not to find criminal traits in Aschenbach:

and, of course, we do find them. Cholera is sweeping through Venice, but the city authorities have done everything possible to suppress knowledge of this fact. Because he can read the German papers, where there are references to it, Aschenbach discovers the truth. He decides that he, too, will suppress it. ' "It ought to be kept quiet," he thought, aroused. "It should not be talked about." And he felt in his heart a curious elation at these events impending in the world about him. Passion is like crime: it does not thrive on the established order and the common round; it welcomes every blow dealt at the bourgeois structure, every weakening of the social fabric, because therein it feels a sure hope of its own advantage...The city's evil secret mingled with the one in the depths of his heart—and he would have staked all he possessed to keep it, since in his infatuation he cared for nothing but to keep Tadzio here.'[14] Later he learns the full extent of the outbreak and of the demoralization it has produced. He considers warning Tadzio's mother to take him and the rest of her family away, but 'he knew that he was far indeed from any serious desire to take such a step. It would restore him, would give him back to himself once more; but he who is beside himself revolts at the idea of self-possession...the thought of returning home, returning to reason, self-mastery, an ordered existence, to the old life of effort...made him wince with a revulsion that was like physical nausea. "It must be kept quiet", he whispered fiercely. "I will not speak!" The know-ledge that he shared the city's secret, the city's guilt—it put him beside himself, intoxicated him as a small quantity of wine will a man suffering from brain-fag. His thoughts dwelt upon the image of the desolate and calamitous city, and he was giddy with fugitive, mad, unreasoning hopes and visions of a mon-strous sweetness...His art, his moral sense, what were they in balance beside the boons that chaos might confer?'[15] This assumption of guilt is immediately followed by the frantic dream-vision in which the erotic content of Aschenbach's soul is turned uppermost, and thenceforward he is 'shattered, un-hinged, powerless in the demon's grip'.[16] Since *Death in Venice* is a story about the artist *in extremis* we may expect his native criminality to step beyond the confines of his art and invade his whole personality, undermining it and turning him into some-thing not very different from a murderer; and this is what happens with Aschenbach. It will not do to suggest that the extermination of his moral sense by passion is something that might equally well have happened if he had not been an artist but a bank manager or a dustman. In the real world this objection would, of course, have substance; but in Thomas Mann's fictional world these isolated and tormented individuals always *are* artists or clearly recognizable artist-surrogates. If a lost story should be unearthed in which Mann does let a bank manager go to pieces morally and mentally to the extent that Aschenbach goes to pieces morally and mentally, you may bet your copy of *Joseph and his Brothers* that the bank manager will play the piano, or have a dark-eyed mother, or—as with Tonio Kröger's banker—write stories. From the point of view of society—this is what Mann says and repeats—the artist is, with his decadence and his passion and his self-obsession, a criminal.

3

The artist is a criminal because he is a decadent: his criminality proceeds from his decadence. It is, of course, not usual to associate crime and decadence: the word 'decadence' has associations quite different from the word 'crime'. But the two ideas *are* joined together in Nietzsche: 'the criminal', he says, 'is a *décadent*'.[17] What does this mean? In what sense can one call the criminal decadent?

Nietzsche's conception is part of his polemic against revengefulness and the desire to punish, which is disguised revengefulness; and it proceeds from his insistence that the criminal is, not 'sinful' and therefore deserving of punishment, but 'sick' and therefore in need of treatment. This may not strike one now as a very remarkable insight (though it is still one upon which few of us are prepared to act, especially in the case of the 'professional' or 'habitual' criminal, i.e. that of the *real* criminal), but taken to its logical conclusion, which is where Nietzsche does take it, this view of the nature of criminality leads to some very remarkable consequences.

Nietzsche's preliminary conclusion (in *Dawn*, 1881) is that the criminal is insane and ought to be handled as a mental patient: 'We have hardly begun to reflect on the physiology of the criminal, yet we have already arrived at the unavoidable insight that no essential distinction exists between criminals and lunatics: provided, that is, we *believe* that the *customary* moral notions are the notions of *mental health*. But no belief is nowadays still so well believed as this one, so let us not shrink from drawing the conclusions of this belief and treating the criminal like a lunatic: above all, not with haughty compassion but with medical skill, medical goodwill...At present, to be sure, he who has received an injury...still wants to have his *revenge* and to obtain it turns to the courts—and these still maintain our abominable penal laws, together with their shopkeeper's scales and their *desire to counterbalance guilt with punishment*: but can we not get beyond this?...Let us rid the world of the concept of *sin*—and send after it the concept of *punishment*!...in early, rude stages of culture, and even now among savage peoples, the sick are in fact treated as criminals, as a danger to the community... here the rule is: the sick are the guilty! And we—are we not yet mature enough for the opposite viewpoint? Are we not yet able to say: the "guilty" are sick?'[18]

Later on, when he has abandoned all thought of 'spiritual causes' and seeks explanations in physiology alone, he no longer refers to the insanity of a criminal but to his general physiological indisposition. In the chapter of *Thus Spoke Zarathustra* called 'Of the Pale Criminal' he gives a broad picture of this conception of the criminal instinct: 'You do not intend to kill, you judges and sacrificers, before the beast has bowed his neck? Behold, the pale criminal has bowed his neck: from his eye speaks the great contempt...He judged himself—that was his supreme moment...There is no redemption for him who thus suffers from himself, except it be a quick death. Your killing, you judges, should be a mercy and not a revenge...You should say "enemy", but not "miscreant"; you should say "invalid", but not "scoundrel"; you should say "fool", but not "sinner"...Thus says the scarlet judge: "Why did this criminal murder? He wanted to steal". But I tell you: his soul wanted blood not booty: he thirsted for the joy of the knife! But his simple mind did not understand this madness and it persuaded him otherwise. "What is the good of blood?" it said. "Will you not at least commit a theft too? Take a revenge?" And he hearkened to his simple mind...then he robbed as he murdered...What is this man? A heap of diseases that reach out into the world through the spirit: there they want to catch their prey. What is this man? A knot of savage serpents

131

that are seldom at peace among themselves—thus they go forth alone to seek prey in the world. Behold his poor body! This poor soul interpreted to itself what this body suffered and desired— it interpreted it as lust for murder and greed for the joy of the knife.'[19]

This approaches the point at which the idea that the criminal is, through the turmoil and contradictoriness of his drives, a type of physiological decadence can be extended to include other types which approximate to him; and this step is taken in *Twilight of the Idols*: 'The criminal type is the type of the strong human being under unfavourable conditions, a strong human being made sick...His *virtues* have been excommunicated by society; the liveliest drives within him forthwith blend with the depressive emotions, with suspicion, fear, dishonour. But this is almost the *recipe* for physiological degeneration. He who has to do in secret what he does best and most likes to do, with protracted tension, caution, slyness, becomes anaemic; and because he has never harvested anything from his instincts but danger, persecution, disaster, his feelings too turn against these instincts —he feels them to be a fatality...Let us generalize the case of the criminal: let us think of natures which, for whatever reason, lack public approval, which know they are not considered beneficial or useful, that Chandala feeling that one is considered not an equal but as thrust out, as unworthy, as a source of pollution. The colour of the subterranean is on the thoughts and actions of such natures; everything in them becomes paler than in those upon whose existence the light of day reposes. But virtually every form of existence which we treat with distinction today formerly lived in this semi-gravelike atmosphere: the scientific nature, the artist, the genius, the free spirit, the actor, the merchant, the great discoverer...I draw attention to the fact that even now, under the mildest rule of custom which has ever obtained on earth or at any rate in Europe, every kind of apartness, every protracted, all too protracted *keeping under*, every uncommon, untransparent form of existence, brings men closer to that type of which the criminal is the perfection. All innovators of the spirit bear for a time the pallid, fatalistic sign of the Chandala on their brow: *not* because they are felt to be so, but because they themselves feel the terrible chasm which divides them from all that is traditional and held in honour.'[20]

The notion that the criminal is a decadent type is here already brought into contact with the notion that the artist is a decadent type, and in Mann's conception of the artist as a criminal type the two notions are fused. Logically this fusion is altogether illegitimate, in fact an elementary logical error: the syllogism 'the artist is decadent, the criminal is decadent, therefore the artist is a criminal' is an example of the 'fallacy of undistributed middle'. But we have seen before that, although he used and needed philosophical concepts, Mann was not well-versed in the practice of thinking philosophically and was, quite simply, not a philosopher; and I do not for a moment suggest that he arrived at his idea of the criminality of the artist by way of a fallacious syllogism. The union of 'artist' and 'criminal' undoubtedly took place below the level of conscious ratiocination. But the very fact — and it is an obvious fact — that Mann *uses* philosophical ideas in his novels and stories but uses them for an artistic and not at all a philosophical purpose is at the very least a strong indication that none of the ideas he uses is or could be original to him, that he has *acquired* his ideas, and precisely those ideas he can make best use of. All I am concerned to do here is to indicate where they came from and to suggest (what would also be indicated by the principle of economy) that they all came from the same source, this being the reason they all *cohere*. I assume, naturally, that the reader of his novels and stories feels some explanation of the provenance of his ideas is called for: or is it normal and a matter of course to regard artists as criminals?

4

The criminality of the artist sounds like a piece of youthful romanticism, but it is not: on the contrary, it is a theme which comes fully and firmly into its own only at the end of the author's life. I do not believe I need to dwell on the criminality of the Devil's disciple, Leverkühn. Contemporaneously with Leverkühn there appears — in chapter 31 of *Doctor Faustus* — the holy sinner and chosen of the Lord, Gregory, whose story is told at such length that the reader must be intended to see in his career a parallel with that of Leverkühn. This legend of the most-outside man as the elect of God appealed so strongly to Mann that he afterwards told it all over again at the length of a medium-size novel. In this novel the artist-as-criminal is for the first time the central theme. It is, indeed, the only theme.

From none of the stories he has told does Mann feel a greater need to keep himself at a safe distance than he does from the story of Gregorius vom Stein. Undoubtedly he, Thomas Mann, is not its author: he tells us so continually. 'Clemens the Irishman, *ordinis divi Benedicti*'[21] is writing it down, and Clemens never lets us forget the fact. Moreover, he writes it in language which no modern author could possibly have employed, an odd, antique-sounding and -looking language, opaque and hard to read. Undoubtedly this is a very ancient work, a manuscript from the very distant past, not the work of a man now living. But even Clemens, the credulous and quaintly-gifted monk, is not the real author of the tale: he is only repeating what has already been written down by the poet Hartmann von Aue in his famous epic poem *Gregorius vom Stein*; Clemens knows of the events he records only at second hand. Not that it should be supposed that Hartmann was himself the real author: he took his story from earlier recitations in the French language and merely transferred them into German; he is no more able to vouch for their truth than Clemens is. Who, then, *is* the originator of *Der Erwählte*, published under the name of Thomas Mann but quite obviously not the work of that urbane and very modern spirit? Let us venture a bold guess and suggest that the hidden hand is that of Leo Naphta. And if anyone should doubt that, with this guess,we have hit the nail on the head, I suggest he show the book to Settembrini, who would recognize at once the mind and manner of that professional obscurantist. The whole work is opposed to, written in opposition to, 'the Enlightenment'; it calls all the Settembrini-values in question; more, it asserts the falsity of these values, it turns its back on clarity, rationality and daylight, and seeks the truth in the dark, the paradoxical, the impossible. It wants to believe in 'sin', it wants a 'miracle of salvation', it *inverts* the judgments of the Enlightenment. It is certainly the work of Naphta.

The first descriptions of Gregory set him firmly in the ranks of the artist-outsider, beyond and set against society. The Abbot who gives him his name considers him 'obviously of far finer metal' than his supposed brother Flann, and is interested in him 'above all because the Abbot knew that he was born in great sin'.[22] Even as a boy, Gregory 'held his head leaned to one shoulder, with his arm bent to the other one, the eyes, hidden under their dark lashes, looked down sideways into a dream'.[23] He learns very easily, but there are certain things in him 'which sometimes even spoiled his taste for monkish learning and for books, in that it seemed to him not only that he was different from his kind in fabric and pattern but also that at bottom he did not fit with the monks and his fellow pupils either...that he was secretly a stranger here as there'.[24] At fifteen and sixteen 'he had grown to be the pleasingest stripling, slender of limb, the face narrow with small straight nose, charming mouth, lovely brows, the face bespeaking a gentle melancholy'.[25] When the poor clod Flann is finally driven to despair by his supposed brother's obvious superiority he shouts at him: 'You are a son of the hut just like me...and still you aren't, it's as though you crawled out of a cuckoo's egg and you're something differnt to us, body and soul.'[26] Gregory attributes his victory over Flann in the ensuing fight to 'a faculty...of extraordinary concentration';[27] later in life he accounts for the continual victoriousness of Duke Roger by saying he 'must have the gift of pulling himself together in a fight, beyond the ordinary measure, and collecting his vital spirit in one burning point',[28] and Maître Poitevin pointedly repeats this explanation: it is a definition of genius, and Gregory is clearly intended to be a natural genius. And yet, because of his origins, he is 'from head to foot...a work of sin and shame'.[29] He goes on to perform acts which, to the mind of the author of his story, ought to bar him for ever from the world of men; he himself feels overwhelmingly conscious of having sinned, and retires to a tiny island where, chained to a rock, he lives out seventeen years of total solitude during the course of which he becomes monstrous. And then he is led to Rome and crowned Pope: 'Heaven...led the child of shame, his mother's spouse, his grandfather's son-in-law, his father's father-in-law, monstrous brother of his own children, to St Peter's seat and was, I well understand, so moved by its own incomprehensibility that the emotion converted itself into the self-acting, mighty swinging and clappering of all the bells of all the seven parishes.'[30] It is the apotheosis of the artist-as-criminal, the most-outside man *come out on top.*

'All election is hard to understand':[31] it is this note which sounds through *Joseph* and into *The Holy Sinner* and, if that work had been completed, we might perhaps have heard it sounding in *The Confessions of Felix Krull*. Certainly, Felix is in a comic fashion 'elect', the favoured of fortune, *der Erwählte*, the man incomprehensibly successful: whether Mann had any unmistakable triumph in store for him which might have redeemed and sanctified, if only in a parodistic sense, the deceit and fraud which constitute his career we cannot say. Erika Mann tells us that not one word more of the confessions was written after the publication of the third part; the work came to a complete halt; so perhaps the author had nothing further in mind for Felix Krull, perhaps the very lowness of the character defeated him. In any event, the criminality of the artist-surrogate and holy sinner Gregory has its comic counterpart in the criminality of the artist-surrogate and successful confidence trickster Felix. Indeed, one hardly needs to speak of Felix as a surrogate: he is virtually an artist *tout simple*. His first taste of success comes from a fraud perpetrated by his father: the pretence that he is an infant prodigy. This suggests to Felix the possibilities opened up by fraud as a way of life, so that from being a fraudulent artist he becomes an artist in fraud, with a strong suggestion that there is very little difference between the two. This suggestion is powerfully reinforced by the episode of Müller-Rosé—one of the key episodes in Mann's work.

Müller-Rosé is a singer and actor whose hold over his public is absolute: 'this whole shadowy assembly [at the theatre] was like an enormous swarm of nocturnal insects, silently, blindly, and blissfully rushing into a blazing fire' when Müller-Rosé inspires them to enthusiasm.[32] He is incredibly immaculate and self-assured, he 'dispensed the joy of life—if that phrase can be used to describe the precious and painful feeling, compounded of envy, yearning, hope, and love, that the sight of beauty and lighthearted perfection kindles in the souls of men'.[33] Felix goes round to Müller-Rosé's dressing-room after his performance: 'I shall never forget the disgusting sight that met my boyish eyes', he tells us.[34] Müller's natural complexion is, in contrast to the rosy appearance he presents on stage, 'cheeselike'; the eye from which the make-up has been removed is 'inflamed and watery'; and his chest, shoulders, and upper arms are covered with 'horrible pustules, red-rimmed, suppurating, some of them even bleeding; even today I cannot repress a shudder at the thought of them'.[35] Felix reflects that 'this repulsive worm is the reality of the glorious butterfly in whom those deluded spectators believed they were beholding the realization of all their own secret dreams of beauty, grace, and perfection!...What unanimity in agreeing to be deceived! Here quite clearly there is in operation a general human need... which Müller-Rosé's abilities are created to satisfy'.[36]

Müller-Rosé belongs to the first part of the *Confessions*, written in 1911, and thus precedes Mynheer Peeperkorn, Cipolla and Adrian Leverkühn, who are his fictional successors, and Mussolini and Hitler, who are his real-life counterparts. It is a very remarkable anticipation. Felix urges the reader to 'ask yourself what it was that impelled this miserable mountebank to learn the art of transfiguring himself every night...Remind yourself how this man could not hear often enough or emphatically enough the assurance that he had truly given pleasure, pleasure altogether out of the ordinary. It was the drive of his heart towards that yearning crowd that made him skilful in his art; and if he bestows on them joy of life and they satiate him with their applause for doing so, is not that a mutual fulfilment, a meeting and marriage of his yearning and theirs?'[37] Yes, it is. And is it not also Hitler and his ecstatic congregations twenty years later? And does Felix's way of looking at it not provide some additional explanation of the ambiguity of Mann's reaction to the nihilistic dictators? Müller-Rosé has nothing to offer the crowd except pure magnetism: everything else about him is fraud, but this magnetism is real—and to the mind of Felix Krull *justifies the fraud*.

It recalls Nietzsche's explanation of the origin of Wagner's histrionic powers: 'When the *ruling idea* of his life—the idea that an incomparable amount of influence...could be exercised through the theatre—seized hold on him, it threw his whole being into the most violent ferment...this idea appeared at first...as an expression of his obscure personal will, which longed insatiably for *power and fame*. Influence, incomparable influence —how? over whom?—that was from now on the question and quest that ceaselessly occupied his head and heart. He wanted to conquer and rule as no artist had done before, and if possible to attain with a single blow that tyrannical omnipotence for which his instincts obscurely craved.'[38] Nietzsche wrote these words when he was pro-Wagner, and the book in which they appeared was intended as support for the first Bayreuth Festival of 1876, but he has been unable to keep out of them a hint, later to be developed mightily in his anti-Wagner writings, that the desire to make an impression constitutes all that is genuine in Wagner's art. Be that as it may, it is not likely to be disputed that the content of Hitler's speeches was fraudulent but the effect they produced was real; and this also applies to the stage personality of Müller-Rosé: his appearance is fraudulent but the effect it produces is real. The realization that this is so convinces Felix Krull that art is a fraud justified by the effect it produces.

During one of his nocturnal excursions into the streets of Frankfurt, Felix inspects and admires the contents of a jeweller's window. Reflecting on the stones displayed there, he remarks that 'these precious structures' are 'essentially quite worthless'. It is merely a passing observation, but it is typical of Felix's way of thinking: wherever he looks he cannot help seeing fraud, while at the same time admiring the fraudulent effect.

Felix becomes an artist very early in life, and not merely an impersonation of an artist. His godfather, 'a greatly admired artist',[39] is named Schimmelpreester, which, as he himself explains, means 'the high priest of mould' (this in the 1954 revision of part one: in 1911 his name was Maggotson, which is less amusing but embodies the same idea); and Schimmel-preester's outlook on life and art exercises great influence over Felix's growing mind. As a youth he poses for his godfather in a wide variety of costumes, and he comes to prefer this make-believe to reality. It goes without saying that he is a 'fanatical lover of music'.[40] Indeed, throughout his childhood and youth he is deeply immersed in his imagination, and the common pretences of childhood are perpetuated into young manhood and then into full adulthood, so that he in fact lives his whole life in imagination, constantly pretending that he is what he is not and that his circumstances are other than they are. 'What a glorious gift is imagination, and what satisfaction it affords!' he exclaims:[41] it is clear that Felix's frauds are, in his own estimation, works of art for which the material is, not words or paint or musical sounds, but his own life.

Felix is certainly an artist: yet he is also equally certainly a criminal, and a criminal in the most commonplace sense of the word. But this 'yet' is not to be found in Felix's confessions: on the contrary, the two states are held to be, not merely compatible, but actually to imply one another. Schimmelpreester tells him the story of Phidias and draws the appropriate moral: 'Phidias,...also called Pheidias, was a man of more than ordinary gifts, as may be gathered from the fact that he was convicted and put in jail for embezzling the gold and ivory entrusted to him for his statue of Athena. Pericles, who found him out, allowed him to escape from prison, thereby proving himself not only an expert in art but, what is more important, an expert in understanding the nature of the artist, and Phidias or Pheidias went to Olympia, where he was commissioned to make the great gold-and-ivory Zeus. And what did he do? He stole again. And imprisoned in Olympia he died. A striking combination. But that is the way people are. They want talent, which is in itself something out of the ordinary. But when it comes to the other oddities that are always associated with it, and perhaps essential to it, they will have none of them and refuse them all understanding.'[42] Than which, one might say, nothing could well be plainer.

7 Sickness

> The nihilistic movement is merely the
> expression of a physiological decadence.
>   NIETZSCHE[1]

I

' "Since I have known the body better," said Zarathustra to one
of his disciples, "the spirit has been only figuratively spirit to
me." '[2] In other words, Nietzsche abandoned faith in
'spiritual causes' and began to seek always the 'physical cause'.
This fact is fairly well known and also fairly well misunderstood:
the misunderstanding is often revealed by the placing of the
word 'mere' or some other deprecatory expression in front of the
word 'physical' or the word 'body'. Nietzsche is then understood
to have become anti-rational and to have proposed setting loose
the passions or the 'will' and letting them trample and override
the dictates of reason. But this is all foolishness and false perspective. The initial problem to which 'physiologism' is an
attempt at an answer is the *origin* of reason.

Where does the thinking mind come from — assuming it is
not a 'gift of God' or a piece of 'the divine' in man? One
is entitled to propose an idealist solution, and say that 'mind' is
what is given, the basis and origin of all things, and the body
is a product of the mind. One is also entitled to propose a
materialist solution, and say that 'matter' is what is given and
mind a product of matter ('the body'). One is thirdly entitled
to declare the problem unsolvable or meaningless. What one is
not entitled to do is to prefer the idealist solution because it
seems more in keeping with the very high opinion one has of
oneself and denounce the materialist solution as immoral. To
look down on the body as if it were something inherently inferior
to 'the spirit' is not only to beg the question but to allow one's
reason to be overborne by one's feelings — that is, to be guilty of
precisely the charge levelled at Nietzsche in this connexion.

Nietzsche's commitment to 'the body' is to be found full-
blown and perhaps over-blown in the chapter of *Thus Spoke
Zarathustra* called 'Of the Despisers of the Body': ' "I am body

and soul"—so speaks the child...But the awakened, the enlightened man says: I am body entirely, and nothing beside; and soul is only a word for something in the body. The body is a great intelligence, a multiplicity with one sense...Your little intelligence..., which you call "mind", is also an instrument of your body, a little instrument and toy of your great intelligence. You say "I" and you are proud of this word. But greater than this...is your body and its great intelligence, which does not say "I" but performs "I"...There is more reason in your body than in your best wisdom. And who knows for what purpose your body requires precisely your best wisdom?...I want to say a word to the despisers of the body. It is their esteem that produces this disesteem. What is it that created esteem and disesteem and value and will? The creative Self created for itself esteem and disesteem, it created for itself joy and sorrow. The creative body created mind for itself, as a hand of its will.'[3]

The conviction that the body produces the conceptions of the mind became rooted in Nietzsche quite early on, and is likely to find expression in the most varied contexts. In *Human, All Too Human* (1878), for example, we read: 'As soon as the origin of religion, art and morality is so described that it can be perfectly understood without the postulation of *metaphysical interference*...the greater part of our interest in the purely theoretical problem of the "thing in itself" and "appearance" ceases to exist. For...with religion, art and morality we do not touch upon "the nature of the world in itself"; we are in the realm of "ideas", no "intuition" can take us any farther. The question how our picture of the world could differ so widely from the revealed nature of the world will then be confidently left to physiology and the history of the evolution of organisms and concepts.'[4] Metaphysics is here considered a branch of physiology. In *Dawn*, certain effects of passion are likewise seen as a branch of physiology: 'An act of violence proceeding from passion, from anger for instance, can be understood physiologically as an attempt to prevent a threatening attack of suffocation. Countless deeds of wantonness and arrogance vented on others have been the diversion of a sudden congestion of blood through a vigorous activity of the muscles.'[5] Later in *Dawn* it is suggested that moral judgments are of physiological origin: 'It is not a good idea to let the evening sit in judgment on the day: for all too often it is weariness that is here judge over strength, success and good will. And one should likewise exercise the greatest caution in regard to *old age* and its judgment of life, especially since old age, like evening, loves to clothe itself in a new and alluring morality and knows how, through evening skies and twilight and a peaceful or passionate stillness, to put the day to shame. The reverence we show towards the elderly man, especially if he is an elderly thinker and sage, can easily blind us to the *aging of his mind*, and it is always necessary to draw forth from their hiding place the *symptoms* of this aging and weariness, that is to say the *physiological* phenomena behind his moral preferences and prejudices, so as not to become fools of reverence and destroyers of knowledge.'[6]

After *Zarathustra*, the physiological origin of thought in general is asserted again and again, as for example in *Beyond Good and Evil* (1886): 'Behind all logic...there stand evaluations, in plainer terms physiological demands, for the preservation of a definite species of life. For example, that the definite shall be of greater value than the indefinite, appearance of less value than "truth": but such valuations as these could, their regulatory importance for *us* notwithstanding, be no more than foreground valuations, a definite species of *niaiserie* which may be necessary precisely for the preservation of beings like us.'[7] Logic is here accorded significance only as the consequence of a certain physiological condition; and in this following passage philosophy is derived from forms of language and forms of language are derived from physiology: 'The singular family resemblance between all Indian, Greek and German philosophizing is easy enough to explain. Where, thanks to the common philosophy of grammar—I mean thanks to unconscious domination and directing by similar grammatical functions—there exists a language affinity it is quite impossible to avoid everything being prepared in advance for a similar evolution and succession of philosophical systems: just as the road seems to be barred to certain other possibilities of world interpretation...: the spell of definite grammatical functions is in the last resort the spell of *physiological* value judgments and racial conditions.'[8]

In the *Genealogy of Morals* (1887), Nietzsche suggests that philologists, historians and philosophers might like to ponder the question 'what light does linguistics, and especially the study of etymology, throw on the history of the evolution of

moral concepts?' But he goes on to say that 'it is equally necessary to engage the interest of physiologists and medical men in
these problems (the problems of the *value* of existing evaluations)
...Indeed, every table of values, every "thou shalt" known to
history or ethnology, requires first of all a *physiological* illumination and interpretation—in any event, it requires this before it
requires a psychological one; and they all await a critique on
the part of medical science.'[9]

The 'physiologizing' process is carried to its completion in
Twilight of the Idols (1888), where, in the section called 'The
error of a false causality', Nietzsche denies the existence of
'spiritual causes' of any kind: 'We have always believed we
know what a cause is: but whence did we derive our knowledge,
more precisely our belief we possessed this knowledge? From
the realm of the celebrated "inner facts", none of which has up
till now been shown to be factual. We believed ourselves to be
causal agents in the act of willing...It was likewise never
doubted that all the *antecedentia* of an action, its causes, were to
be sought in the consciousness and could be discovered there
if one sought them—as "motives": for otherwise one would not
have been *free* to perform it, *responsible* for it. Finally, who would
have disputed that a thought is caused? that the ego causes the
thought?...of these three "inner facts" through which causality
seemed to be guaranteed the first and most convincing was
that of *will as cause*; the conception of a consciousness ("mind")
as cause and later still that of the ego (the "subject") as cause
are merely after-products after causality had, on the basis of
will, been firmly established as a given fact, as *empiricism*...
Meanwhile we have thought better. Today we do not believe
a word of it. The "inner world" is full of phantoms and false
lights: the will is one of them. The will no longer moves anything, consequently no longer explains anything—it merely
accompanies events, it can also be absent. The so-called
"motive": another error. Merely a surface phenomenon of
consciousness, an accompaniment to an act, which conceals
rather than exposes the *antecedentia* of the act. And as for the
ego! It has become a fable, a fiction, a play on words: it has
totally ceased to think, to feel and to will!...What follows from
this? There are no spiritual causes at all! The whole of the
alleged empiricism which affirmed them has gone to the devil!
That is what follows!'[10]

There are no spiritual causes, therefore there are only physical causes: everything derives from the physical condition. If the physical condition is sound, the moral judgment, for instance, will take a certain direction; if it is unsound, moral judgment will take a different direction: the nature of the judgment will be determined by the physical condition. This is the reverse of what is conventionally considered the order of cause and effect: 'The most general formula at the basis of every religion and morality is: "Do this and this, refrain from this and this—and you will be happy! Otherwise..." Every morality, every religion *is* this imperative...In my mouth this formula is converted into its reverse...: a well-constituted human being, a "happy one", *must* perform certain actions and instinctively shrinks from other actions, he transports the order of which he is the physiological representative into his relations with other human beings and with things. In a formula: his virtue is the *consequence* of his happiness...The Church and morality say: "A race, a people perishes through vice and luxury". My *restored* reason says: when a people is perishing, degenerating physiologically, vice and luxury (that is to say, the necessity for stronger and stronger and more and more frequent stimulants, such as every exhausted nature is acquainted with) *follow* therefrom.'[11]

The concept of physical causation is taken very far by Nietzsche. He applies it, for example, to the teachings of Jesus: 'We recognize a condition of morbid susceptibility of the *sense of touch* which makes it shrink back in horror from every contact, every grasping of a firm object. Translate such a physiological *habitus* into its ultimate logic—as instinctive hatred of *every* reality, as flight into the "ungraspable", into the "inconceivable", as antipathy towards every form, every spatial and temporal concept, towards everything firm, all that is custom, institution, Church, as being at home in a world undisturbed by reality of any kind, a merely "inner" world, a "real" world, an "eternal" world..."The kingdom of God *is within you*".'[12] Further: '*Instinctive hatred of reality*: consequence of an extreme capacity for suffering and irritation which no longer wants to be "touched" at all because it feels every contact too deeply. *Instinctive exclusion of all aversion, all enmity, all feeling for limitation and distancing*: consequence of an extreme capacity for suffering and irritation which already feels all resisting, all need for resistance, as an unbearable *displeasure* (that is to say as *harmful*, as *deprecated* by the instinct of self-preservation) and knows blessedness (pleasure) only in no longer resisting anyone or anything, neither the evil nor the evil-doer—love as the sole, as the *last* possibility of life...These are the two *physiological realities* upon which, out of which, the doctrine of redemption has grown...The fear of pain, even of the infinitely small in pain —*cannot* end otherwise than in a *religion of love*.'[13]

One could continue to quote indefinitely, but I think the point is made: Nietzsche derives the phenomena of mental life from those of physical life; and he is consequently vastly concerned—one could even say obsessed—with the question of 'decadence', which, as he employs the term, might be defined as the spiritual consequences of physical decline.

I will not deny that the *feelings* are all against this conclusion: we want to believe in the autonomy of the spirit, and even in that of the feelings which protest at the questioning of this autonomy. And for Nietzsche too the conclusion was not easy: the fierceness with which he asserts it may be attributable to the resistance it needs to overcome. We may even be driven by the strength of our feeling into denying that our feelings in general, and our moral feelings in particular, can *possibly* have their origin in our physiological condition. If this is how we feel, we ought to reflect that there are at any rate some feelings which clearly *do* derive from our physical condition: all those feelings, for example, which have to do with our masculinity or femininity. In this instance the derivation of the spirit from the body is a commonly accepted fact: no one believes that distinctively male and distinctively female attitudes of mind are autonomous operations of the spirit. Little boys are as a rule more violent than little girls, little men more brutal than little women: the reason for this distinction is, as everyone knows, that the former have a male and the latter a female *physiology*. Everyone suspects, even if they do not know, that sexual ambiguity, the inability of an individual to adopt a definitely masculine or a definitely feminine attitude of mind, originates in physical disequilibrium; and the popular ascription of homosexuality to the same cause—so that homosexual men are supposed to be womanish and homosexual women mannish in senses other than the primary sense—may well be accurate and the many apparent refutations of this view no more than instinctive dissimulations prompted by social disapproval of homosexuality. (The Freudian assertion to the contrary—namely, that the libido of a *normally constituted* individual can be directed towards any object—seems to me one of the least likely propositions ever left unproved. Freud—to speak generally—repudiated the soul but invented psycho-analysis, i.e. 'the loosing again of the soul'; Nietzsche repudiated the soul and then repudiated psychology ('the study of the soul') except as a secondary discipline after the resources of physiology had been exhausted.)

If, then, we are prepared to concede that at least some part of our 'spirit' is the immediate product of our body, we shall become more receptive to the suggestion that it all is, that 'spirit' is the name of something in the body. When we speak of an idea, an attitude of mind, as being 'sick', we shall be prepared to consider that this expression is more than a metaphor, that the spirit can be sick as the body can be sick, and perhaps *because* the body is sick. A body that rejects all nourishment and consequently grows pale and thin is pronounced ill without any equivocation: what of a *mind* that does the same? what of a 'heart' that does the same? Are they not ill also? Can one distinguish here, are these things not all the same thing, namely illness, physiological indisposition, a decline of the body? If all absolute values have disappeared in Europe, if the 'spirit' in Europe has rejected everything it has hitherto nourished itself on, may the cause not be at bottom physiological? Is Europe perhaps ill, not in any metaphorical or symbolic sense, but literally, unequivocally ill? The fact is that medical science has not yet attempted any elucidation of the problem: are value judgments biological in origin? The day will come when it will be compelled to do so (the grounds for this assertion will appear in our final chapter). Meanwhile, we have Nietzsche's assertion—purely 'philosophical', that is to say speculative, a hypothesis put forward for investigation—that 'the nihilistic movement is merely the expression of a physiological decadence': that the decline in the belief in truth originates in a decline in the 'certainty' of the body.

2

No subject is more obviously of interest to Mann than illness. I have already felt entitled to speak of an obsession. He had the reputation at one time of being a storyteller whose characters were all invalids: this is, of course, an exaggeration, but a useful one: it tells us something of value about the *general effect* of his work. A 'general effect' will, by definition, ignore details and nuance, and will to some extent misrepresent and falsify; but it will also reveal something true. The word 'Dickensian' is often used in contexts where one can hardly tell what it is supposed to mean; yet the word does have a true and honest meaning, expressing the general effect produced on the mind of a reader of Dickens's novels, and it can legitimately be used to describe some scene or event in life which produces a similar effect: when so used it can tell us in a single breath more of the reality of this scene or event than a thousand-word description or a ten-minute film could. As yet there is no comparable expression 'Mannian', and perhaps there never will be: but if it existed its central idea would be the idea of illness—a 'Mannian situation' would be one in which the behaviour of the participants was, whether they knew it or not, dictated by some form of physiological indisposition or malfunction.

This much would, I think, be obvious even to a merely surface reader: so many of Mann's characters are in some sense sick that the 'general effect' would be unavoidable. But it requires only a little more depth of understanding to perceive that this sickness exists, not for its own sake, not as a sentimental or morbid personal predilection of the author's, but as a means for the production of something else, something which it unfailingly does produce. Let us disclose what that is by comparing the deformed little Herr Friedemann with another deformed character, say Quasimodo. The stories in which these two characters appear might seem to be utterly different, but they both have at their centre the effect produced upon the life and character of a man by the fact that he is physically deformed. Hugo's idea is simple, direct, 'popular': deformity of body produces deformity of mind. Quasimodo is like a tamed animal, half ape, half dog: when his feelings are offended he can revert to savagery. One is given to understand that beneath all this he is 'really' human, and the pathos of his situation is supposed to lie in his inability to communicate with other people on a human level because his deformity revolts them and scares them away; but this is an aesthetic error, tasteless and unnatural sentimentality on a level with Dickens's sentimentalizing of imbecility (Smike): if we pity Quasimodo it is because where one expects humanity he is sub-human and all his emotions are caricatures of human emotions. All this, it is plain, seems to Victor Hugo to go without saying: since his body is deformed, Quasimodo's spirit must necessarily be deformed too, and in the most obvious way. In this he has popular psychology on his side, but he does not have Thomas Mann on his side. For what is the effect of deformity on little Herr Friedemann? It makes him cultured. Excluded from the normal world by his distorted body, he takes refuge in 'the spirit', he becomes artistic, he acquires appreciation for and discernment in the 'things of the mind'. In every respect but one he becomes a finer human being than the people around him (it is that one thing in which he is inferior, of course, which finally destroys him): there can be no question here of 'pitiableness', little Herr Friedemann is certainly not pitiable, his deformity is for him the source of a certain kind of superiority. Deformity of body, by directing the spirit back on to itself, elevates the spirit: that is the assertion of *Little Herr Friedemann*. But—the story goes on to say—it is a perilous elevation, it is not firmly-based, it is not a high rock or a tall building but more like a ladder which one has climbed and continues to climb but which can easily sway and topple—or be kicked away from below: the most valued spiritual states as the *perilously vulnerable* product of the inadequate physique.

3

This, then, from the first, from the very beginning: Herr Friedemann's culture is the product of his deformity. It is culture only of a kind—of the kind produced by deformity; it is not positive, firm, the product of strength; it is reactive, a hiding place, a flight from truth. *Such* a flight is a flight in a circle: when one has flown as far as one *can* fly, there is truth immediately ahead—one has all the time only been flying back to it. Culture of this kind, the product of a bad constitution, is itself ill-constituted; it cannot maintain itself alone, it has no autonomy; it increases only as the body's sickness increases, it is altogether dependent on the body. If the body becomes *too* sick, if a state of morbidity is reached which can truly be called decadence, then the spirit too catches the contagion and becomes sick: it becomes overfull, overripe, yet at the same time more and more hungry, it can never have done with eating and chewing and consuming and then eating again, it will take in anything, it will try to digest anything, it will *sweat* with the effort of its mastication and the pain of its overfullness. In a word, the spirit will become *romantic*. 'The classic I call the healthy, the romantic the sick':[14] did Mann take that famous remark of Goethe's literally? I think he did, and I think he did so under the influence—fully conscious or otherwise—of that idea expressed most clearly by Nietzsche that there are no spiritual causes but only physical ones. If the spirit is sick—overfull, sweating, in pain, romantic—it is because it is the product of sickness; if the spirit topples it is because what is sick must in the end topple: sickness as the beginning and sickness as the end of culture. This is why, of all subjects, none is of greater interest to Man than sickness.

4

We shall examine, again, the decline of the Buddenbrooks. 'Decadence', artistic sensibility and physical indisposition go together, they form a syndrome. Christian is artistic and neurotic in equal measure, and these symptoms of degeneration are attended by physical symptoms: 'It isn't a pain, you know,' he says, 'it is a misery, a continuous, indefinite ache. Dr Drogemüller in Hamburg tells me that my nerves on this side are all too short. Imagine, on my whole left side, my nerves aren't long enough!...I never go to sleep properly. My heart doesn't beat, and I start up suddenly.'[15] He suffers from rheumatism, 'difficulty in breathing and swallowing...and a tendency to paralysis—or at least to a fear of it. He did not look like a man at the end of his thirties. His head was entirely bald except for vestiges of reddish hair at the back of the neck and the temples.'[16] Thomas tells him in an outburst of anger: 'You are a growth, a fester, on the body of our family'[17]—a rather unkind remark, but its imagery is suggestive and sticks in the mind. The author is delineating, not some vague 'spiritual decline', but a decline into sickness.

In Christian Buddenbrook physical morbidity is accompanied by moral uncertainty. When he leaves for Hamburg his departure is 'a heavy loss to the club, the theatre, the Tivoli, and the liberal livers of the town. All the "good fellows"...took leave of him at the station...And Lawyer Gieseke, amidst general applause, fastened to Christian's overcoat a great favour made out of gold paper. This favour came from a sort of inn in the neighbourhood of the port, a place of free and easy resort where a red lantern burned above the door at night, and it was always very lively. The favour was awarded to the departing Chris Buddenbrook for his distinguished services.'[18] The irony is laboured, but that is an effect of the year 1900: the point is that, by the standards of the Buddenbrooks, Christian is immoral and a debauchee; and this characteristic is bestowed upon a man who, it is perpetually insisted, is ill.

The association of physical decline with moral decline is repeated in the case of Thomas. At the high point of his career, Thomas declares that 'just now I feel older than I am', and delivers himself of the opinion that 'the outward and visible material signs and symbols of happiness and success only show themselves when the process of decline has already set in'.[19] At 43 he is 'an old, worn-out man': the muscles of his mouth and cheeks are flabby, his face betrays 'an anguished weariness', his eyes are tired, red and watery, and his mind is filled with 'dull, confused, rambling thoughts'.[20] It is precisely while he is in this condition that he decides to undertake a transaction which he has earlier denounced as unethical but which would be profitable to the firm, thus confirming Christian's remark of many years before that every businessman is a rascal.

Hanno's decadence is associated so closely with sickliness as to be virtually identified with it, so that his artistic sensibility seems to be as directly a product of his physiology as does that of little Herr Friedemann. Hanno almost dies at birth and as an infant he is constantly unwell: 'soon after the christening a three-day attack of cholera-infantum was almost enough to still for ever the little heart set pumping, in the first place, with such difficulty'.[21] He has convulsions while teething. He suffers from 'pavor nocturnus' — night fears and visions. He weeps excessively. His second teeth cause him even more suffering than his first; the extractions required leave him exhausted and are followed by attacks of gastric fever, fitful heart action, giddiness. He is plagued by bad teeth for the whole of his brief life. His skin is very pale and his bodily strength inadequate, the reason being his failure to manufacture a sufficiency of red corpuscles. The medicines he has to take are all horrible except one: arsenic pills, which he is given once and which do him 'a world of good...But however much he asked to have the dose repeated — for he felt almost a yearning for these sweet, soothing little pills — Dr Langhals never prescribed them again':[22] he is, in fact, in physical need of narcotics, and he starts smoking very young. Cuts and bruises take a very long time to heal. He has deep blue shadows about his eyes. Blue shadows about the eyes are in Mann an unfailing sign of artistic sensibility, and bad teeth are an unfailing sign of general physical decay: and since Hanno's mother has the blue shadows and his father the bad teeth, Hanno, as inheritor of both, ought to have counted himself lucky to have survived as long as he did. Enough: Hanno Buddenbrook is loaded with sufficient ailments to kill a family — which, of course, is what they eventually do succeed in doing when they kill *him*.

Buddenbrooks, then, presents us with a vast *programme* of decline: of decline as loss of wealth, of decline as loss of status, of decline as loss of moral certainty and fibre, of decline as 'artistic decadence': but underpinning them all is decline as physiological decay. The Buddenbrook family becomes *sick* — the rest follows.

5

Physical sickness as the originator of the phenomena of the spirit becomes the immediate theme in *The Magic Mountain*. The sanatorium and its inmates have always been taken to represent Europe in its moral and intellectual disintegration: but is more than a metaphor intended? If we answer this question with Yes, the true ground for our answer will lie outside the novel itself, in the very large amount of illness to be found throughout Mann's work before and after *The Magic Mountain*; in those instances in which spiritual states are unmistakably the product of physical disease; and in the conviction we feel that no writer possessing the imagination of Thomas Mann would continue to employ a single metaphor from the beginning to the end of his creative life unless it were something more than a metaphor. But there also seems to be within the novel ample evidence that the spiritual state of the inmates of the sanatorium is as much a product of their physical condition as is Adrian Leverkühn's.

The initial idea is, to be sure, the reverse of this: 'A man lives not only his personal life, as an individual,' the author says, 'but also, consciously or unconsciously, the life of his epoch and his contemporaries...All sorts of personal aims, ends, hopes, prospects, hover before the eyes of the individual, and out of these he derives the impulse to ambition and achievement. Now, if the life about him, if his own time seem, however outwardly stimulating, to be at bottom empty of such food for his ambitions; if he privately recognize it to be hopeless, viewless, helpless, opposing only a hollow silence to all the questions man puts, consciously or unconsciously, yet somehow puts, as to the final, absolute, and abstract meaning in all his efforts and activities; then, in such a case, a certain laming of the personality is bound to occur,...a sort of palsy, as it were, which may even extend over into his physical and organic part.'[23]

This view is approximately the conventional one, and may be compared with that of 'the Church and morality' which say that a people perishes through vice and luxury. But during the course of the novel it is reversed; indeed, it is only on condition that it *is* reversed that the nature of the sanatorium Haus Berghof becomes comprehensible. There are a dozen suggestions, made almost in passing, that it is the physical condition that produces the emotion, the thought, the 'spirit'. Hans discusses with his cousin his heart palpitations and says that 'it is unpleasant to have the body act as though it had no connexion with the soul, and put on such airs—by which I mean these senseless palpitations. You keep trying to find an explanation for them, an emotion to account for them, a feeling of joy or pain, which would, so to speak, justify them...' Joachim replies that it is the same when one has fever: 'there are pretty lively goings-on in the system then too...it may easily be that one involuntarily tries to find an emotion which would explain, or even halfway explain the goings-on'.[24] What is being described here is the familiar phenomenon of unmotivated emotion—a sensation of excitement for which there is no obvious cause. What happens when this happens is that the conventional order of cause and effect is apparently reversed: the physical sensations which are supposed to be produced by the emotional stimulus occur spontaneously, of themselves, and the emotional sensation associated with them *follows*.

Hans Castorp's view of the relation between health and stupidity on the one hand and disease and cleverness on the other has already been quoted. When Joachim, having left the sanatorium, is compelled to return by a worsening of his condition, Hans reflects: 'That is serious. And directly before the manœuvres he has been so on fire to go to. H'm, it's certainly a skin game, it's playing it low down on poor Joachim, it's the very opposite of the ideal. By which I mean that the body triumphs, it wants something different from the soul, and puts it through—a slap in the face of all those lofty-minded people who teach that the body is subordinate to the soul. Seems to me they don't know what they are talking about, because if they were right, a case like this would put the soul in a pretty equivocal light...The question I raise is how far they are right when they set the two over against each other; and whether they aren't rather in collusion, playing the same game. That's something that never occurs to the lofty-minded gentry.'[25] Since the whole sense of what is meant by 'soul' implies the strictest separation of soul and body, this suggestion is tantamount to wanting to abolish the soul.

I believe that, if one assembled sufficient quotations from *The Magic Mountain*, one could make it seem likely that the tendency of the novel is to support the thesis that spiritual effects are the product of physical causes, and that the sanatorium is not a metaphor or symbol but a piece of 'higher reality': Europe is *really* a sanatorium. But this novel is so very full of intellectual ideas—the author's ambition seems to have been to include representatives of *every* intellectual position possible to Western man—that the suspicion would always remain that other quotations could 'prove' it to have a quite different tendency. Much more persuasive than any number of quotations is the plain fact that the magic mountain represents 'the higher regions', namely art, religion and philosophy, and the world below the less exalted spheres of work and everyday life. The image derives from Hegel, and specifically from the 'philosophy of spirit' in his *Encyclopaedia of the Philosophical Sciences*, in which art, religion and philosophy occupy the sphere of 'absolute spirit' at the apex of human activity. The scheme of the *Encyclopaedia* itself suggests a pyramid or mountain rising higher and higher into a more and more rarefied atmosphere, and one could believe that the imagery of *The Magic Mountain* was a direct transference from it. But added to this is something of which there is no hint in Hegel: Mann places upon the mountain a sanatorium and asserts that all those who dwell in these regions are ill. The healthy do not belong there and cannot endure it there: the air is too thin for them. Some 'recover' and return to the flatland (i.e. the normal healthy world): but soon their recovery is seen to be illusory and back they come up to the sanatorium. Some, notably Naphta and Settembrini, can never go down, they are too ill to leave the mountain. Some, notably cousin Joachim, do not really belong up there and are consequently ill at ease, thinking only of the time when they will be able to leave and get on with the real business of life. But to those constitutionally suited to it, notably Hans Castorp, the sanatorium is home, they have no desire to leave, and the real business of life in the plains below grows less and less real to them, until they forget it altogether. It is because these higher regions are accessible and comfortable only to the sick that Hofrat Behrens, who presides over them, must himself be sick. The morbid origin of the 'spirituality' of these mountain-dwellers is the reason this spirituality is itself morbid, unstable, liable to the crassest errors and blunders: sexuality becomes puerile eroticism, *otium* neurotic idleness and the demon Dumps, ingenuity crazes and fads, religion spiritualism, natural assertiveness querulous quarrelsomeness, pride 'affairs of honour'. In the end the 'spiritual values' represented by these invalids disappear: those who can desert the magic mountain to go and fight one another on the plain, and the First World War, the open and public confession and demonstration that the values of European civilization have come to nothing, gets under way.

6

Two of Mann's chief characters are represented as great artists whose gifts are the product of a morbid physiology. The earlier, Gustav Aschenbach, is ill throughout our acquaintanceship with him, and his visit to Venice is an all-but-conscious sur-render to decomposition. When we first encounter him he is 'overwrought', his work is taxing his sytem and he is unable to find relaxation in sleep.[26] His writing is described as an 'enervating daily struggle' with fatigue,[27] and at 40 he has been worn down by this struggle, his career is a 'constant tension',[28] and his dedication to his art is said to have produced 'a nervous fever and exhaustion'.[29] In point of fact, the nervous fever and exhaustion are the original and native characteristics of the author Aschenbach, and his art is a product of *them*, and not the other way round: 'Gustav Aschenbach was the poet-spokesman of all those who labour on the edge of exhaustion; of the over-burdened, of those who are already worn out but still hold themselves upright; of all our modern moralizers of accom-plishment, with stunted growth and scanty resources, who yet contrive by skilful husbanding and prodigious spasms of will to produce, at least for a while, the effect of greatness.'[30] This is the opposite of natural strength and accomplishment and the reason such 'greatness', in Aschenbach and in other of Mann's creations, is sick. The images of disease which crowd the page as Aschenbach moves through the carbolic-reeking streets of Venice are projected from Aschenbach himself: the dissolution of the city into a morass mirrors the dissolution of the artist into an imbecile. In the end, Aschenbach has nothing left of his former values, art and morality have dropped away, and he knows only a sickness of soul which is indistinguishable from a sickness of body. What does he die of? Cholera is all around him and he takes no precautions against it; one may assume, one is invited to assume, that the carbolic-reeking singer passes it on to him; but the point is finally left obscure. Has he perhaps merely *gone over* the 'edge of exhaustion'?

The later morbid genius is, of course, Leverkühn. The con-nexion between Leverkühn's infected state and his talents as a composer is documented as fully as anything in Mann's work and may be taken as definitely established: no reader of *Doctor Faustus* is likely to feel any doubt that Mann intends us to see Leverkühn's morbid condition as the precondition for his genius. He achieves this objective very ingeniously by associat-ing Leverkühn's compositional style with the origin of his disease. A guide who resembles Leverkühn's former teacher Drag-foot, and whose pronunciation of English and French is wittily said to be 'diabolical', conducts him to a brothel; although he leaves this place as virgin as when he went in, Leverkühn has been bewitched by one of the inmates, a dark-haired girl he names Esmeralda and to whom he subsequently returns. She warns him she is infected, but 'he despised the warning and insisted upon possession of this flesh'.[31] As a consequence he too is infected, and it seems he has infected himself deliberately. The girl's name is reduced to a musical cypher and this cypher is woven into the texture of his compositions: 'her name...whispers magically...throughout his work'.[32] One of his songs—a setting of Brentano's 'O lieb Mädel, wie schlecht bist du', a poem naturally associated with Esmeralda—is 'entirely derived' from that cypher, 'and the horizontal melody and vertical harmony are determined and controlled by it'.[33] This procedure, in which the origin of Leverkühn's syphilitic infection is, so to speak, the only thing present, is of course the seed of the dodecaphonic style of composition which Leverkühn is later represented as having invented. As his creative abilities expand he becomes capable of applying this technique on a larger and larger scale, until in his last composition, the daemonic cantata *The Lamentation of Dr Faust*, every feature of a work lasting one-and-a-quarter hours derives from a single twelve-note row. This may seem a rather laborious way of saying that Leverkühn's musical inventiveness originates in a syphilitic infection of his brain; but in *Doctor Faustus* indirection and laboured ingenuity are the rule, and this association of syphilis and musical genius is in fact an example of relative straightforwardness. The technique of Leverkühn's last composition is identical with that of the song 'O lieb Mädel, wie schlecht bist du', and in that song the only element present, in both words and music, is the syphilis-bringer Esmeralda: if this is not supposed to mean that Leverkühn's music originates in syphilitic infection I do not know what it *is* supposed to mean. But, clearly, that is what it does mean. Adrian, the supreme artist among Mann's fictional artists, owes his genius to his infection.

7

The party which follows Hanno Buddenbrook's christening has just finished and the guests are making their way home. 'In the act of leaving, however, and already at the door, Frau Permaneder [née Tony Buddenbrook] turns. She comes back to her brother and kisses him on both cheeks, and says: "It has been a lovely day, Tom. I am happier than I have been for years. We Buddenbrooks aren't quite at the last gasp yet, thank God, and whoever thinks we are is mightily mistaken. Now that we have little Johann [Hanno]…it looks to me as if quite a new day will dawn for us all!" '[34] The irony in this remark, preserved through fifty years and fed by half-a-century's decline of the European family, becomes the basis of an entire short novel, *The Black Swan*. This story, the last Mann completed, is a final demonstration that the most valued spiritual states can be the product of physiological morbidity.

Rosalie von Tümmler, a widow, lives with her son and daughter in Düsseldorf in the 1920s. Her fiftieth birthday is marred by the pains attending menopause. She is a great lover of nature, especially nature in spring, the season in which she was born, and she and her daughter often take walks into the countryside around Düsseldorf. Rosalie's enjoyment of natural beauty is insisted on at length and is, in view of the outcome of the story, all a ghastly irony. Especially does she love the odours of nature. On one afternoon walk something occurs that 'had a suggestion of mockery' about it: they scent the odour of musk, but discover its origin to be a mound of excrement 'seething in the sun' and surrounded by blowflies. This turns out to be a symbol. Now that she has had no mentrual discharge for two months she regards herself as finished as a woman—but the presence in her thoughts of the Biblical Sarah shows that she is not happily resigned to matronhood: she says that the hardest thing of all is for the soul to adjust to a new condition of the body. Her daughter tells her that her feelings will change, because the psychological is 'only an emanation of the physical' and that it is 'the body that moulds the soul'. Her reason for emphasizing this view of things is that she has noticed her mother taking an interest in her son's tutor, an American of 24 named Ken Keaton, in whose presence she becomes 'decidedly vivacious'. Soon she has fallen in love with Keaton: she confesses the fact to herself and calls it 'grotesque' that this should have happened to her at just the time she has become 'an old woman'. Her feelings seem to prove to her that her daughter is wrong to say that the psychological is only an emanation of the physical, because nature is able to 'make the soul flower miraculously'. Her appearance now begins to acquire 'a conspicuous new bloom, a rejuvenescence'; at length she has to confess to her daughter the 'painful but fascinating psychological miracle' that has happened, whereupon her daughter admits she has noticed that 'in a certain phantasmagoric fashion' her mother has come to look like a girl again. Rosalie explains it as 'my soul's struggle to match his youth'. The daughter believes that 'this accursed seizure'—which is how she describes her mother's love for Keaton—is destroying her mother and wants to send Keaton away, but Rosalie will not hear of this: she says it would be to strike nature in the face, an act of disloyalty to nature and 'a denial of faith in her beneficent omnipotence'. Her belief is that Keaton is 'nature's means of working her miracle in my soul'.

Two weeks later 'something extraordinary' happens: Rosalie's menstrual periods resume—a sign that 'beneficent Nature...has blessed my faith', re-establishing 'harmony between soul and body...with the soul proving herself mistress over the body'. Even her daughter is constrained to admit that it is the 'transformation of the indestructible youth of your heart into an organic phenomenon'.

Rosalie, whose 'heart is swollen with happiness and life', believes she can now consummate her love for Keaton, but during the following month she begins to grow weaker and there is 'an ominous, tired-looking blueness under her eyes'. On the day before her next menstrual period she and her son and daughter and Keaton go for an excursion to Holterhof Castle where, in a secret passageway whose 'mouldy air' envelopes them as they go in, Rosalie passionately confesses to Keaton how much she is in love with him. The event is marred by the 'smell of death' in the passageway, and Rosalie regrets that she should have kissed him for the first time 'in this grave'. That night her menstrual discharge reappears 'calamitously' and she is found 'lying in a faint in her blood'. Examination reveals a 'huge tumour' in the uterus and the presence of cancer cells 'entering into full development'. Surgery discloses that all the pelvic organs are infected with cancer: the surgeon's opinion is that the 'whole story started from the ovary—that is, from immature ovarian cells which...after the menopause...begin to develop malignantly'. Rosalie dies, but not before saying that if death had in her case 'borrowed the guise of resurrection...that was not a lie, but goodness and mercy'.[35]

I do not believe this story requires any commentary whatever: at the end of his life as at the beginning, Thomas Mann asserts that it is 'the body that moulds the soul' and that those who think otherwise are, like Frau von Tümmler, deceived.

8 Encyclopaedic

Genesis 39, 7: 'And it came to pass after these things, that his master's wife cast her eyes upon Joseph; and she said, Lie with me.' The twelfth chapter of the Koran is equally direct: 'His master's wife sought to seduce him. She bolted the doors and said: "Come!" '[1] Are these simple statements in need of elaboration? Would you, male reader, find it something quite inexplicable if your master's wife or somebody else's wife cast her eyes upon you and said 'Lie with me'? Would you, female reader, stand baffled before your own conduct if you one day bolted the doors and said 'Come!'? Social form might speak against such behaviour, but would there be anything unnatural in it, anything contrary to the nature of a woman? The author of the thirty-ninth chapter of Genesis and the author of the twelfth chapter of the Koran evidently did not think so, and nor, if I may presume to guess, do you, male and female reader. But the author of *Joseph and his Brothers*—did *he* think so? He opens the sixth chapter of his third part with the familiar words from Genesis: 'And it came to pass after these things that his master's wife cast her eyes upon Joseph; and she said—' but here he breaks off and inserts a parenthesis 101 pages long between 'she said' and 'Lie with me'. In fact, Mut-em-enet, Potiphar's wife, never does get to say 'Lie with me': after three years of all but unendurable silence, she at long last but with speech impeded by a bitten tongue brings herself to lisp out: 'Thleep—with me!'[2] Within that three-year parenthesis between the moment she cast her eyes on Joseph and the moment she lisped out that distorted request she has undergone, to the same degree and for the same reason, the degradation of Aschenbach: like him, she has abandoned every former value, she has nothing left at all except a burning longing indistinguishable from an illness, she can see and think of nothing except this one young man, and she has changed physically in a sense which would, under other circumstances, be attributable to ageing, so that behind her own mask and that of Aschenbach we can glimpse the ambiguously youthful-old features of Frau von Tümmler, whose passion for a young man was the product of cancer of the womb—and all this so that she can say, and yet still not quite say, the natural words 'Lie with me'.

The long inability of Mut-em-enet to say 'Lie with me' even in a less-than-direct manner is not unique to her among Mann's creations. We have already recalled Aschenbach: let us recall two other highly civilized people who experience comparable difficulty. Hans Castorp cannot say 'I love you' to Frau Chauchat. The machinery which has to be brought into play to enable him to communicate this information in some form would be absurdly disproportionate in any novelist who operated on a smaller scale than Thomas Mann. Between the infection and the confession lie more than two hundred pages; Hans has to begin to doubt the rightness of Settembrini's cold daylight civilization and relinquish the values in which he has been brought up; the 'Walpurgis Night' carnival has to be arranged and the daylight world therewith abolished; finally, Hans has to speak in French: *'pour moi, parler français, c'est parler sans parler'*[3] he tells Madame Chauchat; he refuses to address her as *'vous'* because *'cette forme de s'adresser a une personne, qui est celle de l'Occident cultivé et de la civilisation humanitaire, me semble fort bourgeoise et pédante'*;[4] and only then, having rejected the cultivated Occident and humane civilization, can he, *parler sans parler*, bring himself to stammer out *'je t'aime'*.[5] This *'je t'aime'* is the precise equivalent of Mut-em-enet's 'Thleep—with me!'—a natural phrase which cannot be uttered except the utterer undergo a transformation in the sense of abasement, and then still cannot be properly uttered.

Leverkühn's difficulties are slightly different, yet comparable. In chapter 16 of *Doctor Faustus* he writes a letter to Zeitblom in which he tells him, after a very great deal of beating about the bush, that he has been taken to a brothel and met 'Esmeralda'. The letter is couched in a parodistic antiquated style of German. Why? Serenus opines, in the following chapter, that Leverkühn needed the mask of parody in order to be able to tell the story at all, and especially so as to be able to write down the words 'Pray for me', which can thus be made to sound like a joke. Once again, a character finds simple, direct utterance impossible.

Aschenbach, Hans Castorp, Mut-em-enet, Adrian Lever-kühn: very different people, but identical in this, that they cannot bring themselves to a forthright declaration. 'I love you', 'Lie with me', 'Pray for me': simple phrases, expressing natural feelings, but they cannot say them.

Now I suggest—and I do not believe it will be thought a far-fetched suggestion—that the reason all these characters are afflicted with this inability is that the author himself is afflicted with it, that it is Mann himself who cannot say these simple phrases without enormous circumlocution, and even then cannot really say them. The ground for thinking so is partly, of course, the frequency with which the thing happens, but it is also partly that the consequence of its happening is something which Mann finds very congenial in other connexions too, namely inflation of the text. So intimately, indeed, are the two phenomena—incapacity for direct statement and textual inflation—bound up together that it is hard to say, viewing them in isolation, which really is cause and which effect: whether the compulsion to inflate inhibits direct statement, or the inability for directness leads to inflation. Probably, as I shall later suggest, they are both consequences of another underlying cause. In any event, it is clear, to take only one example, that the inability of Mut-em-enet to say 'Lie with me' and the 101 pages of text during which she struggles to do so are allies. Let us consider briefly this textual inflation as it occurs in other contexts.

Some imaginative writers are putters in, some are takers out: Mann is emphatically a putter in. He is a putter in on an enormous, a heroic scale. One feels that his ideal of a novel would be one which contained everything—an unattainable ideal, but no one can accuse him of not having striven for it. But what does it mean when an imaginative writer puts in on this scale?

Mann himself sought to justify his all-inclusiveness by saying he inclined 'to the view that only the exhaustive can be truly interesting'.[6] I shall waste nobody's time in refuting this view: it is obviously false. Is the story of Joseph not just as truly interesting when it is told in Genesis in twelve pages as it is when Mann retells it in twelve hundred? Did Mann himself not find it truly interesting when he read it in Genesis? Is it not possible even that the reverse of this assertion is true, that a truly exhaustive account of anything would exhaust our interest in it, make it into something upon which the imagination had no further room to play and which it consequently deserted? But our objection to this view ought to derive less from its falsity than from the impossibility of acting in accordance with it. For what is exhaustive? A 700-page account of a seven-year stay at a sanatorium? An average 100 pages for every year? Is that exhaustive? There is another famous book which is a 700-page account of *one day*: but is *that* exhaustive? Would a 700-page account of the content of one minute exhaust all that that minute contains? Exhaustiveness is, as a literary theory or programme, an illusion: one can never be exhaustive, one has to select, prefer this to that, leave out — and one has to do this just as unavoidably as if one had *not* opted for exhaustiveness. But what does it mean when an imaginative writer *wants* this illusion, perhaps needs it, perhaps cannot write unless he lets himself think he is putting everything in?

It is already clear that the deferring of a direct statement is only one of the occasions upon which this illusion of exhaustiveness gets the upper hand. The detailed, often minutely detailed description of everyone and everything is in a sense only a convention of the type of novel Mann writes, a piece of tradition: but even here the excess is striking, it always seems we are told much more about a character or a scene than we need to know. One could take instances almost at random. *Felix Krull*, for example, is full of descriptions, of places and people, that seem altogether redundant; virtually every one of the scores of characters in *Doctor Faustus* is delineated in relentless detail; *Joseph* goes beyond all acceptable limits in this regard — one feels here that Mann really is putting in everything he knows, and one's love for the novel is subjected to stern trials by such things as the biography of Mont-kaw, which almost amount to, and are almost as irrelevant as, inset stories. Where, however, the need for exhaustiveness really does threaten to burst the form apart and reveals itself naked and practically unashamed is in the actual encyclopaedic chapters, which would wreck the novels to which they belong if the novels were not so large as to be able to contain them. (In the case of the unfinished *Felix Krull* the encyclopaedic chapters do wreck the novel, in the sense of breaking up the flow of a narrative which is not long enough to reduce them to proper perspective: *Felix Krull* is, as it stands, a series of episodes.) Huge quantities of information are put in, but the result is not knowledge: it is a heap of marvellous data which the reader, following the author's lead, gazes on with exhausted wonderment. Mann is certainly well-informed, but the impression he is supernaturally well-informed fades when one recognizes the same information repeated in different novels (compare the sub-chapter 'Research' in *The Magic Mountain* with Part III chapter 5 of *Felix Krull*, and that again with similar excursions in *Doctor Faustus*). The encyclopaedic character of these chapters overflows into other chapters: the discussions between Naphta and Settembrini are encyclopaedic in as much as the author tries to introduce every subject under the sun; the mythological, Egyptological and Biblical material which forms the encyclopaedic chapters of *Joseph* also forms the substance of much of the dialogue, especially in the earlier parts of the novel; and in *Doctor Faustus* musicology and a deluge of miscellaneous knowledge floods out over the entire book. The psychologizing, the examination of the characters' motives and feelings, must also be considered a product of this encyclopaedic urge: the desire appears to be present to expose every layer of the mind and to examine it from every possible aspect. Now I do not question that much of this is very interesting, even enthralling to read: Mann was, after all, a very successful essayist, and the essayist does not lose his skill when he obtrudes himself into his novels; but that it produces a general sense of too-muchness, of inflation, of the inclusion of more than can be aesthetically justified, I also take to be unquestionable.

Are we in a position to suggest any answer to our twice-repeated question as to why a writer becomes encyclopaedic on this scale and wants to cherish the illusion he is being exhaustive? Certainly we are already in possession of a clue to the answer: it lies precisely in the *illusoriness* of exhaustiveness. However strong an impression it may make upon us and to whatever wide-ranging activity it may lead us, an illusion is always by its nature a negative phenomenon: it is a reaction against that which it replaces, namely the original positive phenomenon. An illusion arises from a refusal or inability to accept reality and is in its nature a rejection of reality and of precisely that part of reality which it is intended to conceal and abolish: the origin of an illusion is to be sought in its anti-thesis. Supposing exhaustiveness to be an illusion, what is its antithesis? Answer: selectivity. 'Exhaustiveness' is the illusion one is not selecting. What, then, does it mean when an imaginative writer needs the illusion he is not selecting? It means, clearly, that he is *incapable* of selecting, that he is in possession of no principle by which he can consciously select. It means that he does not know why he should exclude this and include that, he has no table of values which would tell him whether this is more or less important than that: so he puts them both in, and a third and fourth thing too—he becomes 'exhaustive', he becomes encyclopaedic.

Inability to select rationalized as a faith in exhaustiveness leads to inflation, to too-muchness: is this all it leads to? Inflation could, after all, have been edited out, could still be edited out: would the effect of 'exhaustiveness' thereby be abolished, so that one would no longer need to speak of it? Or are there other, profounder effects that cannot be edited out, effects which extend to the heart of the novels and do not merely condition their most superficial aspect, their size? We must remember that we have not yet discussed, let alone discovered, the *cause* of this inability to select, the reason Mann lacks a principle by which he can consciously include and exclude and distinguish text from commentary. Perhaps if we inquire after these profounder effects we shall come nearer to this as yet undiscovered cause.

Let us examine a well-known passage in *Doctor Faustus* which will prove to be a signpost indicating the way we ought to go. Serenus is discussing Leverkühn's *Apocalypse* oratorio and the impression it has made upon him is such that he cannot describe it without continual resort to a kind of oxymoron: he characterizes its style, for example, as displaying 'a dynamic archaism',[7] and the impression conveyed is of a composition 'pushed to the very limits of musical erudition, technique, intellectuality'[8] which is at the same time overwhelmingly emotional. The *Apocalypse*, we are told, has 'incurred the reproach both of blood-boltered barbarism and of bloodless intellectuality'.[9] Now, on the level at which Adrian represents Germany this is an objective observation, for the Germans have in fact been simultaneously reproached with being blood-boltered barbarians and bloodless intellectuals, and it is only the word 'blood' which makes this judgment seem paradoxical: there is nothing paradoxical about an intellectual barbarian — some, indeed, might think it the correct description of a very prevalent type of modern man. It is also objective on the novel's biographical level, since Adrian's compositional technique is that of Schoenberg and Schoenberg's music is typically characterized by 'barbaric' violence produced by extremely intellectual means (most striking instance: the dance around the Golden Calf in *Moses and Aaron*). But as Serenus goes on he reveals that something more is meant than this easily resolvable paradox. He writes of 'that pandemonium of laughter, of hellish merriment which...forms the end of the first part of the *Apocalypse*' and describes it as a 'sardonically yelling, screeching, bawling, bleating, howling, piping, whinnying salvo, the mocking, exulting laughter of the Pit'. In this passage, he says, 'is revealed to me, in a way to make my heart stop beating, the profoundest mystery of this music, which is a mystery of identity.' What is meant by this phrase is soon explained: 'this hellish laughter at the end of the first part has its pendant in the truly extraordinary chorus of children which ...opens the second part', and this children's chorus 'which has won, touched, and ravished even the reluctant, is in its musical essence...the devil's laughter all over again...The passages of horror just before heard are given, indeed, to the indescribable children's chorus at quite a different pitch, and in changed orchestration and rhythms; but in the searing, susurrant tones of spheres and angels there is not one note which does not occur, with rigid correspondence, in the hellish laughter'. What is revealed here, says Serenus, 'is Adrian Leverkühn. Utterly. That is the music he represents.'[10] What Serenus has described with so much quaking is two passages in which everything is different except the order of the notes: that is to say, he has described the principle of musical variation, of which there are literally countless, probably many millions of examples. In his capacity as Schoenberg, inventor or at any rate first major practitioner of serial composition, Leverkühn has, to all appearances, merely put into practice one of the simplest theoretical operations of that compositional system, namely the exact repetition of the note-row with pitch, rhythm and orchestration changed. I have also read the objection that if everything in the children's chorus is different from everything in the devils' chorus except the order of the notes it would make more sense to say these two choruses were almost completely different than to say they were virtually identical. But these three objections would have weight only if Serenus were becoming excessively or disproportionately excited over a real composition; indeed, the descriptions of Leverkühn's works in *Doctor Faustus* are so detailed, technically exact and musically convincing, in short so well written, that one has in general to remind oneself constantly that not a note of this music exists, that these compositions are imaginary; and if we bear this in mind we shall realize that the apparent order of cause and effect is here the reverse of the real order: in other words, that Mann wishes to make a certain point, advance his narrative in this or that direction, and then, with this objective in mind, fashions the 'composition' accordingly; Serenus then analyses the composition and, not surprisingly, finds in it that which Mann has put there. The procedure is comparable with that of a detective story, in which the detective apparently deduces (properly, inductively infers) facts which are of course in reality known to the author from the outset, the narrative being so fashioned (placing of clues, provision of motive and opportunity, etc.) that the detective shall be able to 'deduce' them. If, then, one is to criticize Zeitblom's analyses of Leverkühn's compositions one can no more go about it as if he were analysing actual compositions than one can criticize a fictional detective as if he were trying to solve a real mystery: all one can do is to argue that the compositions do not really lend themselves to or cannot sustain the interpretation he places upon them — that is to say, that Mann has failed to provide adequate clues. For my part, I think the role assigned to serial composition in the novel, from its earliest employment in the song '*O lieb Mädel, wie schlecht bist du*' to *The Lamentation of Doctor Faust* at the end, is a marvel of ingenuity, and I am quite prepared to let the author employ it here to make a point without carping overmuch at the perhaps too great wonderment of the simple Serenus at what is a not very exceptional procedure. And what is this point? It is, as Serenus has said, the 'mystery of identity': Mann wants to assert that moral opposites are capable of being viewed in such a way that they become united and seem identical: that the devils and the angel children are one and the same.

Adrian's compositions are in general employed as vehicles for demonstrating a union of opposites: 'heat and cold prevail alongside each other in his work', Serenus says in one place: 'sometimes in moments of the greatest genius they play into each other, the *espressivo* takes hold on the strict counterpoint, the objective blushes with feeling'; and this, he says, has 'like nothing else...brought home to me the idea of the daemonic'.[11]

This uniting of opposites which Adrian's compositions embody derives from the science he studied before he deserted it for music, namely theology; so that in a sense his music is a continuation of his theology by other means. His most influential teacher in this department was the sinister Schleppfuss, whose views Serenus himself, who reports them, seems almost to agree with. 'I have already said', he repeats in his main discourse on Schleppfuss, 'that theology by its very nature tends and under given circumstances always will tend to become daemonology.'[12] This is a union of opposites in itself, as well as a pointer to the nature of Leverkühn's compositions, and Schleppfuss's lectures are hardly more than an elaboration of this initial assertion. 'Schleppfuss was a good instance of the thing I mean', Serenus goes on: '...he received, if I may so express myself, dialectically speaking, the blasphemous and offensive into the divine and hell into the empyrean; declared the vicious to be a necessary and inseparable concomitant of the holy, and the holy a constant satanic temptation, an almost irresistible challenge to violation.'[13] Later, Schleppfuss is allowed to become a little more explicit: 'the dialectic association of evil with goodness and holiness played an important role in the theodicy, the vindication of God in view of the existence of evil, which occupied much space in Schleppfuss's course. Evil contributed to the wholeness of the universe, without it the universe would not have been complete; therefore God permitted it, for He was consummate and must therefore will the consummate — not in the sense of the consummately good but in the sense of All-sidedness and reciprocal enlargement of life. Evil was far more evil if good existed; good was far more good if evil existed; yes, perhaps — one might disagree about this — evil would not be evil at all if not for the good, good not good at all if not for evil.'[14] Later still, in expatiating on the meaning of temptation, Schleppfuss is reported as asserting 'the dialectical unity of good and evil..., for holiness was unthinkable without temptation'.[15]

These notions remain fixed in Adrian's head until, in that crucial interview with the Devil, he accords them unequivocal approval: 'Do you believe in anything like an *ingenium* that has nothing to do with hell?' he asks himself. '...Do you ween that any important work was ever wrought except its maker learned to understand the way of the criminal and madman?...Without the morbid would life all its whole life never have survived?...Do we draw the good things out of the nose of nothing?'[16] His 'pact with the Devil', in whatever light one likes to view it, is on the biographical level an acknowledgment of the truth of Schleppfuss's contentions anent the mutual conditionality of good and evil, and the musical compositions which succeed it and, in Adrian's own eyes, are made possible by it, are founded upon this unity of opposites, to which they frequently give patent and *fortissimo* expression.

That good and evil cannot be separated is not a discovery of *Doctor Faustus*: the fact is simply promulgated more openly there. We have already seen it affirmed in Hans Castorp's vision in the snowstorm, a vision in which moral good and evil appear in a very equivocal light. The representatives of beautiful civilization and noble *otium* in that vision seem to him to depend in some way for their existence on the continuance of the horrors going on in the hidden depths of the temple, horrors to which they pay no attention; and when he reflects on the meaning of what he has dreamed he emphatically affirms the rightness of this state of things: 'from love and sweetness alone can form come: form and civilization, friendly, enlightened, beautiful human intercourse—always in silent recognition of the blood-sacrifice'[17]—silent recognition being the same thing as moral indifference. I have already given my interpretation of this vision: that the imagery and meaning come from *The Birth of Tragedy*, where the existence of classical civilization is said to have depended on a sublimation of barbarism and therefore on the existence of barbarism; and this outlook is already 'beyond good and evil' in the sense that it sees something to which that antithesis is no longer relevant. Even more obviously Nietzsche-derived is the figure of Mynheer Peeperkorn. In the sub-chapter 'Vingt et Un' he assumes alternately the antithetical shapes of 'Dionysus and the

Crucified': his habitual incoherence here allows him to utter disjointed phrases identifying himself now with the crucified Jesus, now with the god of wine and unbridled vitality. In Nietzsche's later works Christ and Dionysus are employed as ideograms for antithetical qualities and the reader is invited to choose between them. 'Have I been understood?' he asks at the end of *Ecce Homo*. '*Dionysus against the Crucified*'.[18] It seems likely that the appearance in the person of Mynheer Peeperkorn of precisely these two gods is attributable to the circumstance that Nietzsche set precisely these two over against one another: if so, their union in him is an attempt at a union of opposites in a supra-moral sense—that is to say, a presentation of 'religion' as a phenomenon to which the antithesis 'good and evil' is irrelevant.

In *Joseph*, God is visualized as being essentially beyond good and evil. Very early on we are told that God 'held His tongue and wisely kept silence upon the fact that not only righteous but also evil things would proceed from man'[19] so as to have no trouble from his angelic court. He maintains this prudent silence in face of Abraham's contention that 'if thou wilt have a world, then thou canst not demand justice, but if thou settest store by justice, then it is all over with the world', and the author comments: 'This silence was the expression of a tremendous fact...: the fact that the contradiction in terms of a world which should be living and at the same time just resided in God's greatness itself; that He, the living God, was not good, or only good among other attributes, including evil, and that accordingly His essence included evil...He was not the Good but the All.'[20]

These traits are of course those of Peeperkorn in his capacity as supra-moral god, and as such they are inherited by the Goethe of *Lotte in Weimar*. In the third chapter, Riemer offers us a long explanation of Goethe's power over his contemporaries which reads like a commentary on the Peeperkorn chapters of *The Magic Mountain*. The material Goethe employs for his poems and plays and novels is available to all men, says Riemer, but 'by the addition of *himself*' to whatever material he elects to use he enhances its value 'infinitely'. This addition constitutes the imposition of his personality upon his material; Goethe had called personality 'the greatest gift of God to man', and this mystery of personality is a 'pagan or...nature-mystery' with which modern man 'uplifts himself' now that he has 'lost his taste' for the Christian mysteries.[21] Through reflecting on Goethe, Riemer is led to reflecting on God, with whom he does not shrink from comparing Goethe. God, he says, is 'the whole', consequently his 'attitude is one of all-embracing irony'. He has, he avows, often speculated 'upon the relation between, yes, the unity of the All and the Nothing, nihil', and his speculations have compelled him to 'equate the all-embracingness and the nihilism'. It is wrong to set God and the Devil over against one another: 'the diabolic is only one side—the wrong side, if you like—of the divine'. He concludes that 'heaven looks at you out of one eye, and the hell of the iciest negation and most destructive neutrality out of the other'. This 'horrifying contradiction' is united in 'the gaze of absolute art', which comprises 'absolute love and absolute nihilism and indifference', and that is the 'godlike-diabolic which we call genius'.[22] I can think of a less opaque manner of putting all this, but what at least is clear is that we had no need to wait for the diabolical Schleppfuss to tell us that the divine is beyond good and evil, for here is the innocuous Riemer saying so already, and going on to apply the principle thus invoked to the personality of Goethe himself; for, he goes on to say, Goethe displays in his conduct a degree of tolerance and complaisance which 'depends on the unity of the All and the Nothing, God and Devil, allness and nihilism...amounting to a most peculiar coldness, a crushing indifference'.[23] It amounts to 'an all-embracing irony'. He quotes Goethe's remark that nothing has any savour without irony, and says that 'that is nihilism itself', which he later glosses as 'a destructive tolerance for everything, a world without end or aim, where good and evil both have the same ironic right'.[24]

I have remarked that Mann was inclined to identify with Goethe, but is this not a case of such an identification passing over, by a natural enough process, into its opposite? Is he not here identifying Goethe with Mann, so that the characteristics ascribed to Goethe are actually those of Thomas Mann himself? Is the attitude of mind described in this passage not the attitude which informs all his works, from *Buddenbrooks*, through *The Magic Mountain* and *Joseph*, down to *Doctor Faustus*, *The Holy Sinner* and *The Confessions of Felix Krull*?—namely a 'most peculiar coldness', an 'all-embracing irony', a 'tolerance for everything', the creation of a 'world without end or aim where good and evil both have the same ironic right'? And is this attitude not 'nihilism itself'? Have we not here, as it were suddenly and unexpectedly, come upon the answer to *all* our questions about Thomas Mann? an answer that includes the answer to our question whether his inability to select had any profounder effect, and whether we might discover the *cause* of this inability if we discovered this profounder effect? but which also provides a profounder answer to the questions we have asked earlier on: why his reaction to the authoritarian dictators was so ambiguous, why he sought a philosophy which would furnish him with proof that the artist was a decadent and one that would show him that the artist was a criminal, why ultimately he must see all things through the spectacles of irony, why when he looks for hope he is driven to the mythological, why he despaired of spiritual causes and looked always for the physical cause, why he thought the 'higher regions' must be a product of sickness? Are we not now driven back to the beginning, to the nihilism of the European continent and to Nietzsche's analysis and prophesy with respect to this nihilism? Why does Thomas Mann have no principle by which he is able to select? Because everything has the same ironic right to exist—because this world is not ordered and rational but chaotic and meaningless, above all because there is no 'moral world-order' which would be the guarantor of moral values and thus supply an ordering principle for life. Everything may exist or not exist—it is in this that the 'irony' of its 'right' to exist consists—because there is no *moral absolute* to assert that this has a right to exist and that no right. God himself—Mann's ironical God, that is—has no moral preferences, he chooses both good and evil, he sees no distinction, his ambition is 'universality', all-inclusiveness: he has, indeed, no alternative, for when he lost the capacity for *moral* choice he lost the capacity to *choose at all*, he must perforce 'choose' to be exhaustive—no wonder his attitude towards the products of this 'choice' is an all-embracing irony! The decline is catastrophic: the God who once had his Chosen People now cannot choose at all, the God who once indited 'the Scriptures' now compiles an encyclopaedia. Thus the God fashioned by Mann in his own image: a God who does not know why anything that *can* exist *should not* exist, a God without the power to select. No moral values, therefore no values at all; no moral 'truth', therefore no truth at all; no way of knowing whether anything is of more worth than anything else, therefore no power to prefer, reject, select: the advent of a world without end or aim, the world of nihilism—*that* is what it means when an imaginative writer puts in on the scale Thomas Mann puts in.

The whole world of Thomas Mann's fiction is erected on this basis of no values. It is because this world has no values that the major novels are so long (no principle of selection); it is because it has no values that its ideological tendency is so uncertain (no instinctive moral judgment); it is because it has no values that its *most valuable* inhabitant, the artist, is inverted into a decadent and criminal (the identity of the best and the worst); it is because it has no values that it is seen ironically (self-defence against the meaningless); it is because it has no values that it resorts to mythology (an attempt to create value); it is because it has no values that its only reality is physical reality and its only causes physical causes, and when it tries to account for the fact that it has no values it seeks the explanation in physiology. But because the world which this fictional world seeks to mirror *really has no values*, this fictional world is a *true* mirror and the image it reflects a true image. The aesthetic faults we have discovered in it, which are true faults, are thus in the long run faults in the subject which it reflects. Or, as the mirror replied to the monster: 'There is nothing wrong with me, it is *you* who are distorted'.

2

Long novels are not all long for the same reason. *War and Peace* is long because its author had a long story to tell and one whose spatial vastness made a vast novel the appropriate vehicle for its telling: the size of the novel matches the size of the events it describes. Proust's novel is long because of the minuteness of its analysis of recollection and feeling, which requires a lot of words. *Some Came Running* is long because its author wanted to write the longest novel. *The Magic Mountain*, however, is long for the same reason *Ulysses* is long: an unrealizable ambition for 'universality', for all-inclusiveness. But *Ulysses* is patently and famously a product of its author's loss of his religious faith. He has lost 'the truth', so he clings all the more determinedly to 'the facts': if one collects *enough* facts — who knows, perhaps they will give birth to the truth? For this is a rule without exceptions: he who knows 'the truth' disdains 'the facts', they can be only an irrelevance, an unnecessary burden, perhaps even a danger; but he who has lost 'the truth' seeks it again in the only place it might be found — he flies to 'the facts' as to his last refuge, he heaps them up around him, in the end perhaps he even worships them as the last surviving attribute of his vanished God: 'God is not truth', he says to himself, 'God is facts'.

Over the past 400 years the minds of Europe have been trying to draw the correct conclusion from the loss of belief in the God of truth. Descartes still believed in him, but Spinoza already did not. He lost his faith in the God of Abraham, Isaac and Jacob, and at once flew to the God of the opposite extreme: 'God is not this or that', he said, 'God is this *and* that, he is infinite and has created everything an infinite intellect is capable of conceiving; also he has an infinite number of modes of being' — in short, everything that *can* exist *does* exist and *should* exist: every possibility is a *realized* possibility. God as an infinite collection of facts ('modes of being') was perhaps an inevitability once God as a discrete being had ceased to be believable: the right historical moment had to appear before the realization could come that, if God is everything in general, he is nothing in particular; and, since we cannot know generalities but only particulars, if God is nothing in particular he is nothing at all.

'You believe in God,' said Nietzsche, 'but I tell you you have killed the god you believe in. He is dead. He has become nothing. When you realize that there will be a collapse of values and morale of a kind the world has not seen before — I call that state of things "nihilism", the belief in nothing. Out of this nihilistic state and as a consequence of it there will arise a desire for a new basis for values. I advise you against inventing a new Supreme Being similar to the old: for he will only come to the same end. I advise sticking to the real Supreme Being, namely yourselves, mankind. I teach you the superman.'

At present we are still in the trough, and almost certainly we have not yet reached its lowest point. I admit that the generation which produced Stalin, Auschwitz and Hiroshima will take some beating; but the radical and universal consciousness of the death of God is still ahead of us; perhaps we shall have to colonize the stars before it is finally borne in upon us that God is not out there. Psychologically we are still at the 'God is facts' stage, the stage which began when Spinoza thought he could rescue the Supreme Being by making him coextensive with everything and when the decline in knowledge of 'the truth' led to the demand for an Encyclopaedia. The nihilism of contemporary Europe, the loss of values which made the abyss of the 1940s possible, was a preliminary, perhaps a precipitancy: Hitler, who possessed no moral values, still had to pretend to possess them (he even had to pretend to believe in God). But the day will come when a leader who speaks in moral terms will no longer be understood: it will be the day on which the radical meaninglessness of life has at last become a part of the general consciousness of mankind; in terms of universal history, the end of the theocratic age, the age in which the moral law continued to exist because of a belief, however attenuated at the last, that it was given by God.

3

It is to such sombre reflections as these that one is led through reading the novels and stories of Thomas Mann. Is there anything further, anything perhaps a little less sombre? Yes, there is one consideration which offers a slightly brighter prospect than the prospect of a long decline into universal nihilism. Let us reflect on the most common type of occurrence in Mann's fiction—I mean physical sickness.

I have already tried to show that the sickness which figures so largely is not symbolic but actual, that it is not intended to stand for something else—'spiritual sickness' for instance—but exists in itself. That this is a fact may appear more likely if we consider how uncertain an effect is produced by what clearly *are* intended as symbols. *Buddenbrooks*, for example, opens and closes with a religious ceremony of a sort: how many readers notice this? and if they do, what can they make it mean? Hans Castorp's cigars seem to possess a symbolic significance of some sort: he finds he cannot enjoy them at the high altitude of Haus Berghof, he discusses the fact a great deal with Ziemssen, then gradually his taste for them returns. I am sure the author attached a meaning to all this, but I cannot be sure I have grasped it. The symbolism of the lead pencil, on the other hand, is not so much obvious as rammed down your throat: yes, you say as you read on, I get it, I get the point—but the 'point' continues to be jabbed into you. The black swan in *Die Betrogene* seemed to the translator of that story so significant he adopted it as his title: but either that significance is altogether banal (i.e. death) or it has altogether eluded me—in either event it is an instance of an unconvincing use of symbolism. Now, compare these instances with what some readers of Mann consider also to be a symbol: the physical illness which plagues his characters. It is at once clear that we are dealing with two different things: the effect on the reader of Hans's cigar is incomparably weaker than the effect on him of the fever and consumption with which everyone in Haus Berghof is infected— so much weaker that, if the cigar is a symbol, the fever and consumption is not. And this consideration, I would main- tain, applies to every story in which illness figures: if the Buddenbrooks' barely-remarkable religious ceremonies are symbols, their nervous illnesses, bad teeth and typhoid fever are not; if Frau von Tümmler's black swan is a symbol, her cancer of the womb is not. The symbols are often vague in meaning or all too obvious, and in any event employed with an uncertain touch: the illnesses are part of the basic structure, not merely of this or that story, but of the whole work from *Little Herr Friedemann* to *The Black Swan*.

If, then, it is the case that illness in Mann's work is not meant to symbolize decadence but is intended as a literal equation of decadence and physiological morbidity, it means that Mann joined with Nietzsche in being deeply doubtful of spiritual causes and consequently of any likelihood that the nihilistic decline is going to be arrested by spiritual means. But since spiritual means have so far proved utterly inefficacious to 'improve' the human race in any lasting sense, perhaps Nietzsche and Mann are right to be suspicious of them. Nietzsche certainly and, as I would argue, Mann very probably, came to think that a change in European man which would be a lasting change and not a temporary and at bottom illusory one must be, with whatever degree of subtlety— perhaps with a degree of subtlety of which we have at present no conception—a *physical* change. Indeed, the contention that there are no spiritual causes but only physical ones must unavoidably lead to the conclusion that all change is physical change, whether it appears to be so or not, because there is no other kind of change.

Physical change—that means biological change. There was a time when thoughts of improving mankind biologically in any sense other than making it more resistant to disease were utopianism and science fiction: that time has gone. Today it is possible to speak of the biological improvement of mankind while still keeping one's feet on the ground: the science of the physical modification of man now exists. I believe the hesitancy and reluctance with which anyone has hitherto ventured to speak of this subject has come, not from any universal faith in 'spiritual causes', but from the impossibility hitherto of relating the concept of 'physical causes' to any practical activity. The science of modifying mankind by spiritual means is as old as records: priest and schoolmaster, if not members of the oldest profession, are members of the next oldest, and in most countries it is against the law not to hand over one's children to them for modification by spiritual means. Hitherto, however, the science of modifying mankind by physical means has been limited to the science of medicine, a science whose foundations were until yesterday hardly firmer than quicksand and bog, and whose failings were, unlike the failings of education, instantly detectable. The progress of science has not been even along the whole front, and physics has got well out ahead, as might have been expected from the relative slightness of the resistance it has met. What past stage of the science of physics the science of biology has now reached is hard to say because the rate of development in all the sciences appears to be constantly accelerating: one would suggest it had not yet reached the age of Rutherford if that were not taken to imply that another fifty years must pass before the biological equivalent of nuclear fission can be expected. But whatever stage it has reached—and certainly it is still at a very early stage—it is without question under way, and the whole temper of our era, the cast of our mind and our instinctual priorities and preferences favour its *rapid* advance.

There is no need to emphasize the risks and dangers attending this advance: the newspapers and the clergy—in close alliance, as usual—do that for us whenever even the minutest step forward is made. Journalists whose lives seem otherwise to be altogether free of moral doubt or dilemma begin to agonize over 'enormous moral problems' as soon as human biology is touched on. They are 'sincere', of course; we will allow them that; what we will not allow them is any competence in the sphere of morals. That someone *now*, when European morality has been broken down and, along with everything else, thrown into the crucible—that someone at precisely *this* point of time should publish his fears, prejudices and inherited perspectives in the naive belief he is uttering ethical admonitions —*there* is an 'enormous moral problem' if you like! Of course there are dangers in the new biology, frightful dangers: it hides within itself an abyss into which mankind could *fall*. No one can fail to feel that much of what it promises is novel in a way that nothing has previously been novel, that the changes it will make possible will be radical in a sense that will give a new meaning to the word radical. But no one is in a position to predict what the ultimate consequences will be if these promised changes come about, and certainly not (Heaven help us!) the *moral* consequences; in the very worst event mankind will be in some way or other destroyed; but in the best it will be rendered antiquated, something superseded, an ape—that much we *are* in a position to predict. Let us, for once, be optimistic: let us call our hopes probabilities—this is what being optimistic means—and, setting aside the idea that every radical change must be a change for the worse, that mankind is necessitated to error (the view of the moral leader-writer), let us reflect on what the *happiest* outcome of the new biology could be within the predictable future.

In his luridly-titled but soberly-written book *The Biological Time-Bomb*, Mr G. R. Taylor—a popularizer of science with the rare virtue of not losing his nerve in face of the hair-raising—lists what he believes to be the most likely technical achievements in biology before 1975, between 1975 and 2000, and after 2000. The probability that his judgment is sound is established by the fact that his earliest predictions were fulfilled between his writing them down and their publication in 1968 and that others have been fulfilled between 1968 and the present date. One may have one's reservations about some of them: in a few cases the dates seem *over*-optimistic, and in a few others the achievement seems otiose and unlikely to be carried forward into practice; but on the whole one is very grateful to Mr Taylor for the conciseness of his summary and the persuasiveness of his arguments. One is convinced, by him and by knowledge from elsewhere, that the achievements he describes are theoretically possible now and will become practically possible at some future date.

What are these achievements? Although Mr Taylor does not arrange them in this way, they seem to me to fall into three categories: the control of human reproduction, the extension of healthy human life, the modification of the human mind. In my view, the third category possesses an absolute value, the first two ultimately possess value only in so far as they can finally be subsumed under the third. The ultimate purpose and objective of human biology within the foreseeable future must be the modification of the mind in the sense of enhancing its intelligence.

So far as control of reproduction is concerned, biology has already provided the contraceptive pill; it is at this moment engaged on the first practical attempt at the test-tube fertilization of a human egg and the implantation of the fertilized egg in a womb: these are preliminaries to what will be the decisive achievement in this field: the creation of an artificial placenta and therewith the dreaded 'baby-factory'. Now, there are two possible views about the baby-factory as such: one is that mankind has the obligation to lay hands on 'nature' and direct it according to mankind's best interests, so that the baby-factory is morally possible; the other is that mankind has not even the right to lay hands on nature, so that the baby-factory is morally impossible. Of these two points of view, the former is now in the ascendant: man now lays hands on nature on every occasion nature gives him the opportunity; the shudder of awe without which primitive man could not so much as drive a ploughshare into the earth is something utterly unknown to modern man—modern man *rapes* nature with only the faintest breath of a suspicion crossing his mind that he might be doing something impermissible. That being so, the baby-factory is on its way almost as surely as night follows day: the question is not whether we shall have it, but what it can be made to mean to us when we get it. The sense that the babies made there are *artificial* babies will be the first thing to go: whether a baby is made inside a woman or inside an artificial reproduction of a woman makes no difference to the baby as such: it is still a baby, an infant human. Once that fact has been accepted, the remainder of the problems will fall into perspective, for they are mainly grounded in the fear that baby-factories could produce only government-controlled robots. Indeed, it may be said that the idea of the 'factory' itself is a product of the fear of state control rather than the fear of gestation outside the body as such, i.e. a product of the assumption that the artificial placenta would *necessarily* be a state monopoly. This fear is, of course, not groundless: but is it not exaggerated? The artificial placenta, when it arrives, will be a piece of hospital equipment: you may if you wish call an establishment housing these devices a 'baby-factory' so long as that does not lead you to forget that the babies born there have a father and a mother. The placenta itself may be state-owned, but the baby growing within it will be the product of a fertilized egg, and the real problem is whether *this egg* is state-owned. I can see no reason to suppose it *must* be.

In conjunction with easy contraception and 'test-tube' fertilization, the artificial placenta will remove from the half of the human race which at present bears it the burden of reproducing mankind every generation. What this relief will mean is not easy to imagine. That it will produce 'sexual equality' is the merest beginning, the *first* effect. Half of mankind is at present typically dependent, exploited, kept down: the true underdeveloped country is woman. That will be all over with. At the point at which men and women are at present really unalike, therefore unequal, they will no longer be unalike: their roles in reproduction will be identical. Once that is the case, try persuading women it is exclusively *their* duty to sacrifice career, inclination, 'full development of the personality', 'widening of the consciousness', or whatever, in order to raise children: you will not be able to persuade them so, because it will not be so. They do it now because they are so enormously more involved with the process of reproduction than men are: but they will not do it then. An incalculable amount of fresh intellectual energy will be released upon the world—and *not* in the form of 'feminine competition'! The neuroticism of that concept will be altogether lacking because its origin in a reactive self-assertion to which the 'female instincts' do not entirely assent will be lacking. What else will be all over with? The abysmal flattery of men to which women at present feel themselves compelled; their abysmal subjection to the life-style and -pattern of the man; the abysmal conflict in their soul between sexual desire and sexual fear; the time- and energy-consuming demands of that decorativeness imposed on them by their status as second and subordinate sex; the hysteria engendered by the conflict between the intellect and the child-bearing and -feeding machine: all over and done with. Oh, we shall have some enormous moral problems, don't you worry!

Extension of healthy life: to this sphere belongs the replacement or regeneration of diseased or worn-out organs, the inducement of prolonged coma or hibernation, the control of the ageing process and prolongation of youthful vigour, ultimately the indefinite postponement of death. In no sphere are the immediate consequences of the new biology so obviously beneficial or the ultimate consequences so drastic. A humanity which could double its lifespan would become a new species; a humanity which could secure for itself a life of indefinite length would become a new type of being. The English classic on this subject is, of course, *Back to Methuselah* (the immortal Struldbrugs in the third book of *Gulliver's Travels* are the embodiment of ironical reflections on old age, not on immortality).

Shaw's play is grounded in two unargued hypotheses: that men can live for an indefinite length of time by wanting to (by an act of will), and that longer life will of itself produce an increase in intelligence. The former hypothesis is an extreme example of a belief in 'spiritual causes' and is incredible: there is simply no evidence to support it. One does not need to examine the Lamarckian theory of evolution from which it is supposedly derived to be convinced of its untenability: the concept of 'will' of which Shaw was in possession before he concerned himself with Lamarck and which made Lamarck's theory attractive to him is a misunderstanding and the weakest part of his 'philosophy'. The 'philosophy of will' which, so far as the nineteenth and twentieth centuries are concerned, originated with Schopenhauer, has been a confused mixture of fruitful insight and mind-darkening error. In Schopenhauer's own philosophy, 'will' is the metaphysical ground of being — this is what the word means, its definition, in his use of it. The metaphysical situation of man is that of the embodiment of the will at a stage at which it becomes for the first time conscious of itself and thus capable of knowledge of itself: this knowledge leads to self-repudiation on ethical grounds and, in the man who embodies this self-repudiation of the will, the acceptance of personal annihilation.

Wagner had already anticipated something of Schopenhauer's conclusions before he was confirmed in them by reading *The World as Will and Idea*. His *Nibelung's Ring, Tristan and Isolde* and *Parsifal* give dramatic form to the Schopenhaueran conception of the ethically reprehensible nature of the will and its 'redemption' from existence through self-knowledge. In *Tristan* and *Parsifal* the will appears at what Schopenhauer had called its most intense focal point, namely sexuality, the drive through which the will most powerfully asserts its continued existence: in these two operas the central characters are led, via the torments of sexuality, to the knowledge that the will is the source of all evil and that death—their own death (*Tristan*) or the death of desire (*Parsifal*), which is metaphysically the same thing—is the only positive good because it is the only thing which effectively puts an end to the otherwise enduring ethical evil. In the *Ring* Wotan represents 'will', and the drama is his slow acquisition of self-knowledge, to the point at which he 'wills' his own annihilation—i.e. ceases to will. Wagner followed Schopenhauer's conception of the will with a consistency obscured only by the erotic power of his music, which audiences find far too enjoyable to acquiesce in the notion it represents something that ought to be denied.

The only other influential follower of Schopenhauer to accept this conception as it stood was Deussen, who followed Schopenhauer's lead in equating the philosophy of 'denial of the will' with the teachings of Indian metaphysics and devoted his very considerable talents to translating and expounding the Sanskrit scriptures. Deussen belonged to Nietzsche's generation, and although it was only in this generation that Schopenhauer became a figure of the front rank, its more speculative minds had already directed his ideas into channels which took them very far away from the parent stream. Eduard von Hartmann, a thinker who certainly cannot compare with Schopenhauer for subtlety or intellectual consistency, none the less had the one great inspiration of his life when he called Schopenhauer's will 'the unconscious' (*Philosophy of the Unconscious*, 1869, eight editions by 1879) and thus, although without really meaning to do so, threw all the emphasis of the 'philosophy of will' on to the proposition that the origins of human conduct are to be discovered, not in the intellect, but in the sub-intellectual 'unconscious' region of the 'will'. Von Hartmann's success opened the way for acceptance of the 'philosophy of the unconscious' of Freud, in which Schopenhauer's conception of the primacy of the will is, so to speak, domesticated, and his 'focal point' of the will, sexuality, taken for the nature of will in general.

While these developments were going on, Nietzsche, who also started from Schopenhauer but soon struck out on his own, had come to think that the will as the metaphysical ground of being was on a par with God in being unknowable and thus a concept without content; that where one had spoken of a 'will to live' one should speak rather of a 'will to power', inasmuch as the desire for aggrandizement was capable of overriding the desire to preserve one's existence; that the term 'will' was a description, not of a discrete entity, but of a multiplicity of drives which entered consciousness as it were threaded and knotted together and were thus accorded a single name; that the nature of these drives which had been summed up in the word 'will' had been thoroughly misunderstood in the sense of positing a 'psychical region' of the organism from which they were supposed to proceed, whereas the existence of this region could no more be demonstrated than could the existence of the will; that the (then infant) science of psychology was, although useful as a mode of description, fundamentally misleading as to the nature of the things described; that all psychological phenomena ('spiritual causes') were really physical phenomena, that 'psychology' was really the soul-superstition in scientific disguise, and that the science of the future was physiology. In Nietzsche, the 'philosophy of the will' went through half-a-dozen variations and was at length rejected as false—and all this *before* it had flooded out over Europe and inundated a score of different regions of that continent.

Viewed soberly, the notion of 'will' is an atavism, and resembles a revival of the belief in magic: to believe that 'will' can cause anything is to believe in the existence of a supernatural agency. This is true even if you call the will an '*élan vital*' or 'life-force', and its truth becomes obvious if you make it effective in preventing an organism from growing old. For what *is* 'growing old'? Hardening of the arteries and — a phenomenon of the same sort — degeneration of the vital organs, their loss of ability to keep themselves in working order. Shaw *reacted against* the 'materialism' of the nineteenth century, and his reaction carried him so far that he was at last incapable of acceding to the well-nigh self-evident proposition that a physical effect most probably has a physical cause — that if the physical fact of aging can be prevented it can most probably be prevented by physical means.

Will has meant a large range of things since it was moved into prominence by Schopenhauer, but it has seldom meant anything so silly as the belief that you can prevent your arteries from hardening simply by very much wanting to. We must reject this hypothesis of *Back to Methuselah*, not because we believe the will cannot achieve that much, but because there seems to be no such thing as will, at least not in the sense that one could speak of it as a force or a faculty, as an effective agent, something that *does something*. As for the second hypothesis — that longer life will of itself produce an increase in intelligence — probability seems to be in its favour, but, since no man has yet retained his faculties even for as long as 100 years, there can be no dogmatizing on the matter. Yet it would be surprising if a man of 300 in sound physical shape did not possess a *little* more sense than he possessed at 30; it would be surprising if the extension of the normal expectancy of life to 300 years did not produce a total revolution in human affairs; and if the normal man could expect to live indefinitely until cut off by the inevitable accident or by his own hand — it would be surprising if that state of things did not transform the earth into something we are not now remotely capable of imagining. And that is what is coming, almost as surely as night follows day: *not* because we 'will' it, but because the new biology is even now discovering ways of *preventing the decay of the body*. Physical means for a 'spiritual' end, longer life for a better intelligence: and let us note — for we are still in our euphoric-optimistic mood — how well the advances in the new biology sustain and support one another: for it goes without saying that the great extension of life without efficient contraception would produce a 'population explosion' of some force, to put it mildly.

And now we touch the tenderest, the trickiest, and the most vital spot of all: direct modification of the mind by chemical means. Here our conviction that there are no spiritual causes but only physical ones meets the stiffest opposition – not least from within ourselves – but also offers the firmest ground for hope. Intelligence, memory, desire – *only* chemistry? It is in this 'only' that our oldest inherited habit speaks: we are habituated to looking down on the chemical as on something containing the least amount of 'soul'. But suppose this oldest habit of ours were no more than a piece of childish romanticism, the longest-lived remnant of the foolishness we began to throw off when we recognized our kinship with the animals – namely the idea that what has a demonstrable origin can have no value? But when we became convinced that mankind had evolved from the animal world and was not a special creation, did that make Shakespeare any less *valuable* to us? Was *Lear* not still *Lear* even though its author was a higher form of animal and not a lower form of angel? And suppose intelligence, memory, desire *are* of chemical origin – will Shakespeare not still be Shakespeare? Will we not think, love, fear, hope just as before? For all these things will be just what they were – except that we shall be able to *control* them more. And it is in fact fairly well established that *memory* is chemical; in the field of mind-expanding drugs we are already in the infantile stage: we have them but we do not know how to use them. But the masterpiece in this department – predicted by Mr Taylor, perhaps over-optimistically, for the present century – will be the enhancement of *intelligence* by chemical means: the 'intelligence drug'. Hitherto this has, of all things, seemed the most impossible: but some now living may live to see it a reality. I can think of nothing within prospect which would have so shattering an effect on human life. All our 'problems', the enormous moral ones included, would disappear if the average IQ were raised a mere ten points during the course of a generation. If it were doubled...but that thought is not thinkable, that thought belongs among the things of which we are not yet capable. *Chemical* intelligence? – but what does it matter where intelligence originates, provided only we discover its origin and use our knowledge to increase it?

For mankind must become more intelligent. That is its only hope: because only if it becomes more intelligent will it be able

185

to perform that task which it is at present not intelligent enough to perform: the creation of a new basis for values. The old basis has gone and a new one is not yet in sight: and we are moving down into that state of no values which we have been calling nihilism. Somehow or other we must get off this slide, but as yet we do not know how to. Perhaps we shall go all the way to the bottom, if there *is* any bottom. But perhaps the new biology, frankly dedicated as it is to the proposition that 'spiritual' effects are the result of physical causes, will be able to halt us. Let us for once permit ourselves to think so.

4

In his *Phantasie über Goethe*, Thomas Mann criticized the ending of Goethe's novel *Elective Affinities*, in which a future resurrection is promised the dead lovers Eduard and Ottilie, as 'nothing but a *konzilianter Schnörkel*' — nothing but a conciliatory flourish. It is an interesting criticism, not only because it is valid, but also because it describes a little weakness of his own. *Buddenbrooks*, an account of irreversible decline, ends with a brief expression of religious hope. *The Magic Mountain*, a description of the intellectual and moral confusion of modern Europe, ends with the words: 'Out of this universal feast of death [the First World War], out of this extremity of fever, kindling the rain-washed evening sky to a fiery glow, may it be that Love one day shall mount?'[25] *Doctor Faustus*, the mirror of nihilism, has several endings: the final one is an echo of the ending of Leverkühn's last work, *The Lamentation of Dr Faust*: 'For listen to the end,' Serenus begs us, 'listen with me: one group of instruments after another retires, and what remains, as the work fades on the air, is the high G of a cello, the last word, the last fainting sound, slowly dying in a pianissimo-fermata. Then nothing more: silence, and night. But that tone which vibrates in the silence, which is no longer there, to which only the spirit hearkens, and which was the voice of mourning, is so no more. It changes its meaning; it abides as a light in the night.'[26] One can understand the need, at the conclusion of a long and, it may be, finally spirit-wearying labour, to turn the eyes away, to 'lift' them, to allow oneself the relaxation of a barely-justified hope: but is the result not just what Mann said it was at the end of *Elective Affinities* — a *konzilianter Schnörkel*? And can it be that, through reflecting on Thomas Mann, we have been led unaware into imitating him?—that our talk of the new biology and the prospects it opens out for mankind has also been no more than a *konzilianter Schnörkel*...?

References

1 European Nihilism

1 For Mann and Luther's wedding, see Erika Mann: *The Last Year* (1958) p. 9. Erika Mann transposes the chronological order of Wagner's Luther sketch and the *Meistersinger*
2 Foreword to the one-volume ed. of the English trans. of *Joseph and his Brothers* (1948), p. vii
3 *The Will to Power*, section 598
4 ibid., preface 2
5 ibid., preface 4
6 ibid., section 2
7 ibid., section 617
8 *The Gay Science*, section 125
9 ibid., section 115
10 ibid., section 109
11 *The Will to Power*, section 12/A
12 *On the Genealogy of Morals*, part III section 25; see also *The Will to Power*, section 1/5
13 *The Will to Power*, section 1/3
14 ibid., section 4
15 ibid., section 3
16 *Twilight of the Idols*, chapter IX section 5
17 *The Will to Power*, section 55
18 ibid., section 9
19 *On the Genealogy of Morals*, part III section 28
20 *Erlass über die Bildung des Deutschen Volkssturms*, 25 September 1944, reprinted in Walter Hofer: *Der Nationalsozialismus. Dokumente 1933–1945* (1957), p. 252
21 Reprinted ibid., pp. 85–6
22 *The Will to Power*, section 24
23 *Friedrich und die grosse Koalition* (1914)
24 *Das dritte Reich*, quoted in Ronald Gray: *The German Tradition in Literature, 1871–1945* (1965), p. 52. I found the section on Mann in this study suggestive in many ways

2 Ideology

1 *Friedrich und die grosse Koalition*
2 *Doctor Faustus*, p. 299

3 Reprinted in Joseph Wulf: *Literatur und Dichtung im Dritten Reich. Eine Dokumentation* (1966), p. 24
4 ibid., p. 458
5 *The Genesis of a Novel*, p. 131
6 Quoted in the *New York Times*, 18 June 1950
7 *Buddenbrooks*, pp. 515–16
8 ibid., p. 534
9 ibid., pp. 354–5
10 ibid., p. 132
11 *The Magic Mountain*, p. 160
12 ibid., pp. 155–7
13 ibid.
14 ibid., p. 241
15 ibid., p. 244
16 ibid., p. 245
17 ibid., p. 396
18 ibid., p. 464
19 ibid., p. 185
20 ibid., p. 299
21 ibid.
22 ibid., p. 240
23 ibid., p. 371
24 ibid., p. 466
25 *Doctor Faustus*, p. 242
26 *The Magic Mountain*, pp. 97–8
27 ibid., p. 411
28 ibid.
29 ibid., p. 441
30 ibid., p. 448
31 ibid., p. 697
32 ibid., p. 522
33 ibid., p. 377
34 ibid., p. 380
35 ibid., p. 384
36 ibid., p. 386
37 ibid., pp. 397–8
38 ibid., p. 690 for Naphta, p. 710 for Settembrini
39 ibid., p. 496
40 *The Birth of Tragedy*, section 25
41 ibid., section 12
42 ibid.
43 ibid., section 13
44 ibid., section 15
45 ibid., 'Essay in Self-Criticism', section 2
46 ibid., section 1

47 *Twilight of the Idols*, chapter II, section 4
48 ibid., sections 9 and 10
49 *The Magic Mountain*, p. 592
50 ibid., p. 612
51 *Mario and the Magician*, in *Stories of Three Decades*, p. 538
52 ibid., p. 559
53 ibid., p. 529
54 ibid., p. 535
55 ibid., p. 541
56 ibid., p. 544
57 ibid., p. 545
58 ibid., p. 553
59 ibid., p. 563
60 ibid., p. 551
61 ibid., pp. 547–8
62 ibid., p. 552
63 ibid., p. 555
64 ibid., p. 556
65 ibid., p. 561
66 *The Genesis of a Novel*, p. 60
67 *Doctor Faustus*, pp. 30–1
68 see, e.g., ibid., pp. 175, 481, 482

3 Decadence

1 Quotations from Arthur Schopenhauer: *Essays and Aphorisms* (Penguin 1970), pp. 155–8
2 *The Gay Science*, section 85
3 *Twilight of the Idols*, chapter IX section 22 (what Nietzsche literally says is that Plato maintains this, but he obviously agrees with him)
4 ibid., chapter X, section 5
5 *The Anti-Christ*, section 17
6 ibid., section 2
7 *Buddenbrooks*, pp. 137–9
8 ibid., p. 227
9 ibid., p. 238
10 ibid., p. 250
11 ibid., p. 253
12 ibid., p. 282
13 ibid., p. 283
14 ibid., p. 250
15 ibid., p. 370
16 ibid., p. 372
17 ibid., p. 468

18 ibid., pp. 524–5
19 ibid., p. 600
20 *Tonio Kröger*, in *Stories of Three Decades*, p. 98
21 The last words of 'Ivy Day in the Committee Room' in *Dubliners*
22 Preface to *Stories of Three Decades*, p. vi
23 *Tonio Kröger*, in *Stories of Three Decades*, p. 87
24 ibid., p. 86
25 ibid., p. 93
26 ibid., p. 96
27 ibid., p. 97
28 ibid.
29 ibid., p. 98
30 ibid., p. 103
31 ibid., p. 108
32 ibid., p. 110
33 ibid., p. 128
34 ibid., p. 130
35 ibid., p. 132
36 *Tristan*, in *Stories of Three Decades*, p. 139
37 ibid.
38 ibid., p. 137
39 ibid., p. 135
40 ibid., p. 155
41 *Doctor Faustus*, p. 220
42 *Buddenbrooks*, p. 413
43 ibid., p. 593
44 ibid., pp. 595–7
45 *The Magic Mountain*, p. 113
46 ibid., p. 38
47 ibid., p. 40
48 ibid., p. 164
49 ibid., p. 219
50 *Doctor Faustus*, p. 9
51 *Tischreden* (1566)
52 *Buddenbrooks*, p. 407
53 Preface to *Stories of Three Decades*, p. vii
54 *The Blood of the Wälsungs*, in *Stories of Three Decades*, p. 297
55 ibid.
56 ibid., p. 315
57 ibid., p. 316

4 Irony

1 *The Anti-Christ*, section 7
2 *The Invisible Writing* (1954), pp. 373–4

3 *Tobias Mindernickel*, in *Stories of Three Decades*, p. 52
4 ibid., p. 53
5 ibid., p. 56
6 ibid., p. 57
7 *Buddenbrooks*, p. 598
8 *Doctor Faustus*, pp. 474–5
9 *The Black Swan*, p. 126
10 *Doctor Faustus*, pp. 475, 479
11 ibid., p. 476
12 ibid., p. 478
13 ibid., p. 483
14 ibid., p. 485
15 *The Magic Mountain*, p. 19
16 ibid., p. 538
17 ibid., p. 548
18 *The Black Swan*, p. 5
19 *Tristan*, in *Stories of Three Decades*, p. 144
20 *Little Herr Friedemann*, in *Stories of Three Decades*, p. 4
21 ibid., p. 5
22 ibid.
23 ibid., p. 6
24 ibid., p. 21
25 ibid., p. 12
26 ibid., p. 18
27 ibid., p. 22
28 *Tonio Kröger*, in *Stories of Three Decades*, p. 131
29 *The Dilettante*, in *Stories of Three Decades*, p. 28
30 ibid., p. 29
31 ibid., p. 30
32 ibid., p. 31
33 ibid., p. 35
34 ibid., p. 37
35 ibid., p. 46
36 ibid., p. 48
37 *Gladius Dei*, in *Stories of Three Decades*, p. 191
38 *Tonio Kröger*, in *Stories of Three Decades*, p. 100
39 ibid., p. 99
40 *The Magic Mountain*, p. 92
41 *Confessions of Felix Krull*, p. 296
42 *The Wardrobe*, in *Stories of Three Decades*, p. 73
43 ibid., p. 74
44 ibid., p. 77
45 *Buddenbrooks*, p. 334
46 ibid., p. 551
47 ibid., p. 545

48 *Death in Venice*, in *Stories of Three Decades*, p. 379
49 ibid., p. 380
50 ibid.
51 ibid., p. 427
52 ibid., p. 389
53 ibid., p. 390
54 ibid., p. 392
55 ibid., p. 393
56 ibid., p. 412
57 ibid., p. 409
58 ibid., p. 432
59 ibid., p. 434
60 *The Magic Mountain*, p. 27
61 ibid., p. 83
62 ibid., p. 86
63 e.g. ibid., p. 118
64 ibid., p. 597
65 ibid., p. 146
66 ibid., p. 312
67 *Faust* I, 'Walpurgisnacht', line 34; *The Magic Mountain*, p. 324
68 *The Birth of Tragedy*, section 3
69 *The Magic Mountain*, p. 497
70 *The Birth of Tragedy*, section 3
71 *The Magic Mountain*, p. 709
72 *History of Germany since 1789*, part 10, chapter 4
73 *Doctor Faustus*, p. 173
74 *The Way to the Churchyard*, in *Stories of Three Decades*, p. 79
75 ibid.
76 *Buddenbrooks*, p. 561
77 *The Holy Sinner*, p. 2
78 *Joseph and his Brothers*, p. 241
79 *Confessions of Felix Krull*, p. 39
80 ibid., p. 123
81 ibid., p. 235
82 ibid., p. 244
83 *The Magic Mountain*, p. 220

5 Myth

1 *Beyond Good and Evil*, section 68
2 *On the History of Religion and Philosophy in Germany* (1834), book 3
3 *Joseph and his Brothers*, p. 30
4 ibid., p. 47
5 ibid., p. 620

6 ibid., p. 388
7 *Lotte in Weimar*, p. 223
8 ibid.
9 ibid., p. 250
10 ibid., p. 247
11 ibid., p. 229
12 ibid., p. 270
13 ibid., p. 233
14 ibid., p. 157
15 ibid., p. 177
16 ibid., p. 121
17 ibid., p. 146
18 ibid., p. 123
19 ibid., p. 249
20 ibid., p. 256
21 ibid.
22 ibid., p. 315
23 ibid., p. 338
24 ibid., p. 340
25 *A Weary Hour*, in *Stories of Three Decades*, pp. 294–5
26 *Twilight of the Idols*, chapter IX, section 49
27 ibid., chapter VIII section 4
28 Eckermann: *Conversations with Goethe*, 3.5.1827; quoted by Nietzsche in *David Strauss*, section 1
29 *Twilight of the Idols*, chapter IX, section 44
30 ibid., section 49

6 Crime

1 *Doctor Faustus*, p. 236
2 *Little Lizzie*, in *Stories of Three Decades*, p. 58
3 ibid., p. 61
4 ibid., p. 64
5 ibid., p. 68
6 ibid., p. 61
7 ibid., p. 69
8 ibid., p. 61
9 *Tonio Kröger*, in *Stories of Three Decades*, p. 105
10 ibid., p. 117
11 *The Infant Prodigy*, in *Stories of Three Decades*, p. 173
12 ibid., p. 180
13 ibid., p. 176
14 *Death in Venice*, in *Stories of Three Decades*, p. 419
15 ibid., pp. 429–30
16 ibid., p. 431

17 *Twilight of the Idols*, chapter II section 3
18 *Dawn*, section 202
19 *Thus Spoke Zarathustra*, part I, 'Of the Pale Criminal'
20 *Twilight of the Idols*, chapter IX section 45
21 *The Holy Sinner*, p. 2
22 ibid., p. 68
23 ibid., p. 71
24 ibid., p. 73
25 ibid.
26 ibid., p. 81
27 ibid., p. 90
28 ibid., p. 105
29 ibid., p. 118
30 ibid., p. 205
31 ibid., p. 174
32 *Confessions of Felix Krull*, p. 32
33 ibid., p. 31
34 ibid., p. 33
35 ibid.
36 ibid., p. 35
37 ibid., p. 36
38 *Richard Wagner in Bayreuth*, section 8
39 *Confessions of Felix Krull*, p. 8
40 ibid., p. 21
41 ibid., p. 15
42 ibid., p. 25

7 Sickness

1 *The Will to Power*, section 38
2 *Thus Spoke Zarathustra*, part II, 'Of Poets'
3 ibid., part I, 'Of the Despisers of the Body'
4 *Human, All Too Human*, section 10
5 *Dawn*, section 371
6 ibid., section 542
7 *Beyond Good and Evil*, section 3
8 ibid., section 20
9 *On the Genealogy of Morals*, part I, note
10 *Twilight of the Idols*, chapter VI section 3
11 ibid., section 2
12 *The Anti-Christ*, section 29
13 ibid., section 30
14 Eckermann: *Conversations with Goethe*, 2.1.1829
15 *Buddenbrooks*, p. 332
16 ibid., p. 366

17 ibid., p. 264
18 ibid., p. 266
19 ibid., p. 352
20 ibid., p. 384
21 ibid., p. 346
22 ibid., p. 501
23 *The Magic Mountain*, p. 32
24 ibid., p. 72
25 ibid., p. 500
26 *Death in Venice*, in *Stories of Three Decades*, p. 378
27 ibid., p. 381
28 ibid., p. 383
29 ibid., p. 388
30 ibid., p. 385
31 *Doctor Faustus*, p. 155
32 ibid.
33 ibid., p. 191
34 *Buddenbrooks*, p. 330
35 Quotations from *The Black Swan*, *passim*

8 Encyclopaedic

1 Translation by N. J. Dawood (Penguin 1956), p. 40
2 *Joseph and his Brothers*, p. 769
3 *The Magic Mountain*, p. 336
4 ibid., p. 341
5 ibid., p. 342
6 ibid., p. vi
7 *Doctor Faustus*, p. 377
8 ibid., p. 376
9 ibid., p. 376
10 ibid., pp. 378–9
11 ibid., p. 178
12 ibid., p. 99
13 ibid., pp. 99–100
14 ibid., p. 103
15 ibid., p. 105
16 ibid., p. 236
17 *The Magic Mountain*, p. 496
18 *Ecce Homo*, chapter IV section 9
19 *Joseph and his Brothers*, p. 28
20 ibid., pp. 286–7
21 *Lotte in Weimar*, p. 53
22 ibid., pp. 63–4

23 ibid., p. 65
24 ibid., p. 66
25 *The Magic Mountain*, p. 716
26 *Doctor Faustus*, p. 491

Index

Index